Infinite Mind

Infinite Mind

*An exploration of psi and the capabilities
of the human mind*

Kim Forrester

Published in New Zealand by Kim Forrester Consulting.
www.kimforresterconsulting.com

ISBN 978-0-473-61545-1 (softcover POD)
        978-0-473-61544-4 (softcover)

Cover image by kevron2001, iStock by Getty Images
Cover Design by Kim Forrester
Printed and distributed by BookBaby

This book is dedicated to my greatest loves,
Todd, Daniel
and Sarah ("Are you happy now?").

And to a great explorer, pioneer and man.
Vale, Dr. Edgar Mitchell.

Contents

Acknowledgments		**ix**
Introduction		**xi**
1	PROLOGUE	1
2	A STRANGE AND INTENSE DREAM	9
3	A SILENT FORCE	16
4	QUIET EPIPHANY	22
5	THE CLEAR AND INSISTENT THOUGHT	31
6	BUCKLE IN TIGHT	36
7	TO BE AN ARTIST	45
8	THE SUDDEN AWAKENING	54
9	A HEAVY VOID	65
10	A SENSE OF DREAD	77
11	CONNIE'S HUNCH	86
12	A DETERMINED FUTURE	92
13	THE CHOSEN ONE	102
14	WHO IS DEAD IN THE WHITE HOUSE?	112
15	"I SAW HER TOO!"	125
16	JESSE COULDN'T RESIST	132
17	ANGRY MIST AND THUNDEROUS NOISE	139
18	GRILL FLAME	149
19	INSTINCTIVE AND UNFATHOMABLE	160
20	AN EXCEPTIONAL MAN	174
Tips and Tools		**184**
Notes		**188**
Selected References		**192**

Acknowledgments

I would like to extend my heartfelt gratitude to those who took the time to share their personal experiences with me. Jasmine Beaudoin, Mat Beeche, Dr. John Demartini, Edwina Gleeson, the late Dr. Edgar Mitchell, Jacqueline Harrison, Hannah Hempenstall, Mary Grace Montealto, Matt Omo, Kevin Oxley OAM, Mel Riley, Lou and Ingrid Whittaker and 'Ellie' Wright. I am humbled by your generosity of spirit; I am honoured by your support.

I am also indebted to those who helped transform a collection of stories into a published book. My wonderful editor, Shelley Kenigsberg for her gentle and wise advice; Hannah Hempenstall for setting this project in motion; Larissa Gorsuch, Leigh-ann Dam and Brigid Gibson for their loving insights; Michelle Kuek for her valuable industry contacts. Special thanks also to Gracia, my fairy.

This book would not be possible without the dedicated work of psi researchers around the world. I would like to extend my gratitude to those who continue to expand our scientific knowledge of human capability, with special thanks to Dr. Dean Radin and the team at IONS.

Finally, my deepest love and gratitude goes to my loving, forgiving and hilarious family. Todd, Daniel and Sarah, you are the best of me.

Introduction

History shows that the ability to accept new discoveries is not, generally, something humans do well; it does not sit comfortably with our need to feel powerful and in control. However, as a part of nature, we are inherently programmed to evolve. As much as we resist change or ignore progress, we will always find ourselves propelled forward into glorious unknowns.

I was raised in a fairly regular, flippantly-Christian New Zealand home where spiritual encounters were neither shunned nor encouraged, but I can't claim to have had any particularly mystical experiences in my childhood or youth. I didn't see spirit faces in the window; I didn't have premonitions of impending catastrophe or angelic visitations in my bedroom.

For many years I did enjoy the company of an imaginary herd of horses but, even in my child mind, I knew they weren't real. They fulfilled my desperate desire for a pet horse and a need to belong. For me, life revolved around the experiences of my five physical senses and my rather active and all-consuming imagination.

Now, armed with hindsight and the information in this book, I see how my childhood was also influenced by another, more intangible sense. For many years, I was driven by extreme self-doubt and an obsessive need to make others happy. I was unable to tolerate conflict and anger, and still can't, because it reverberated through my body like a shock wave. I often doubted others' motives; I sensed an underlying falseness behind their smiles. I was desperate to rescue others and make them praise me or laugh because it was the only time I felt truly comfortable.

No doubt there were psychological reasons for my behaviour but I realise now that these characteristics were also the result of my deep connection with the emotions and intentions of others. I'm not speaking of mere empathy, although that was a natural by-product of my experiences. I *felt* people. I absorbed their pain, their anger, their joy and their wickedness. I knew that behind many of those socially acceptable smiles ("I'm fine, thanks.") lingered rage, grief or depression. As a child it made me neurotic. As an informed adult, it serves me incredibly well.

Of course, even if I had been aware that a sixth sense was part of my childhood experience, I would never have claimed any mystical abilities. Even well into my twenties, I believed that psychics *saw* their powerful messages; they saw visions and pictures and apparitions in crystal balls and candle flames. Compared to fabled clairvoyants, feeling others' emotions didn't seem particularly noteworthy.

From a very young age, I was fascinated with topics that lay just beyond the limits of conformity. As a young child, I remember poring over my grandmother's book about unexplained phenomena. I loved astrology and cosmology and felt compelled to learn more about our enigmatic universe. I read horoscopes and fantasy novels and revelled in the idea of other 'unseen' worlds. By the time I was a teenager, I was dabbling in lunchtime Ouija boards with my giggling, nervous friends.

All the while, I remained completely oblivious to the notion that maybe, just maybe, I was drawn to the mysteries of our universe because of an unconscious need to discover more about the mysteries of myself. I was 16 when a fairground mystic told me I was psychic. I remember laughing at the absurdity of his statement. It took 10 years before my curiosity got the better of me, and I decided to test his hypothesis.

I was 26 years old, when I decided to educate myself in things spiritual and mystical.

It began in the comfortable home of a local spiritual teacher in Rotorua, New Zealand. For those first few years, I was determined to be psychic, to receive clairvoyant messages in multi-coloured splendour and float away on visually stimulating meditations. I was ready, I was primed and I was very, very eager to succeed.

The only problem was, I was useless. Terrible. Utterly and completely incompetent.

I began with meditation, but I was quickly distracted by everyday thoughts — what I had for dinner, or how to deal with the current crisis at work. My 'psychic messages' consisted of hunches or ridiculous visions. "I see broccoli,"

I said to a classmate one evening. "Did you have broccoli for dinner?" I added hopefully.

It was many years before I eventually learned something magical about myself. Despite my desire for psychic visions — to see auras and replicate the deeds of traditional clairvoyants — my sixth sense worked in other ways.

I rarely saw any visions (I still very rarely do) but, oh, how the feelings would flow! How intense and incredible the emotions in my body could be. How clear and loud my inner voice could speak — words, names, instructions. My mind and my heart provided me with all the intuitive guidance I needed. I was not a strong clairvoyant but, as my child-self had demonstrated, I was naturally attuned to people and situations through emotion and thought.

This understanding — that I could do things my own way — was a revelation for me. Until then, I had never been told that was possible or acceptable.

As my intuitive abilities strengthened, so too did my belief that psychic insight is not a 'gift' but an aptitude. I was sure that my (by now, quite accurate) ability was not mystical or divinely bestowed. I saw it as an inherent aspect of being human, conscious and part of the universe.

My resolve was cemented when I came across a tiny statistic: 4.6%. Two little numbers; four keystrokes on my keyboard and the key to a wondrous understanding about the universe we call home. This number, 4.6%, is the estimated amount of the universe that humans can measure and understand.[1]

From that moment on, I became passionate about the unknowable — the truths that human minds cannot fathom. Yet I felt these truths resonate with me, intuitively, and I wanted to find a way to convey them to others so they would make better sense.

I immediately began to read, study and absorb all the scientific research I could about psychic ability, consciousness and the universe. (There is plenty!) And I began to write about them, teach them, tell stories and offer examples about them to anyone who was interested.

As I studied, I realised that if we are ever to fully understand who we are and what we are capable of, we need to bring together the latest understandings of spirituality, science and psychology. We need to free ourselves of the need to be right — to know it all and have all the answers — and eagerly explore and accept new discoveries when they present themselves.

It is in this spirit of bold inquisitiveness and fearless evolution that this book has been written. I hope that in the following pages you find something that feeds your intellect, ignites your curiosity and encourages you to take a leap beyond the confines of your conscious mind and into the realms of infinite possibility.

1

Prologue
Kidapawan, The Philippines

The shadows were growing long in Kidapawan. Gracia reclined lower into the bus seat and rested her head wearily against the window. It was a four-hour bus ride from Cotabato City on Mindanao's southwest coast to Davao City on the eastern shore. Kidapawan was only halfway along that journey.

It had been a tiring week for Gracia. She had started her college course in catering and hospitality only two months earlier and for several days she had been undergoing intensive on-the-job training in Cotabato City. Now, she was heading back to Davao for a day off; tomorrow she would turn around and endure the four-hour trip back to Cotabato.

Even for a resilient and energetic 16-year-old, this hectic pace of life was draining. The Weena Express bus to Davao was not busy that day, and she was able to secure herself an entire double seat near the back of the vehicle. It was a rare, restful way to spend the long journey

At just after 2:30pm there was a quick stop in Kidapawan. Just enough time for passengers to alight with their luggage and for any ongoing passengers to climb aboard. By Gracia's estimates they should be back on the road by 3pm and arrive in Davao just as the sun set.

Davao was not a safe place to be after night; unrest and terrorism had been strangling the southern Philippines city for the past few years. So, Gracia was keen to get there by nightfall and ensure she was home, safe, by early evening.

The diesel engines of the bus spluttered into silence as they arrived at the crowded terminal. Around her, passengers began stuffing luggage and shuffling out of seats with the relaxed disorder of the Philippines. *I would really love something to eat.* The thought materialised, uninvited, in Gracia's brain. *Hmm, yeah, I could really do with some food right now.*

The thought was clear, persistent, but Gracia's tired body refused to cooperate. It was so rare to have the use of an entire double seat and she was not keen to risk losing it for a later, probably crowded, bus. Besides, she was used to travelling the full journey without food and a later departure would mean that she would arrive in Davao City after dark. *No,* she thought. *I'll stay where I am.*

But something piqued her senses. The smell of durian wafted into the bus from the stalls outside. The pungent sweetness of the prickly fruit filled her nostrils and teased her taste buds. *Oh, I really, really want some durian.* The

2

yearning was too great; it made her defy her weary body as it insisted she relinquish her comfortable seat.

In a moment of impulse, Gracia grabbed her belongings — a simple paper shopping bag — and sprung toward the front door of the bus. She would have to catch a later ride; to heck with the consequences. She stepped from the bus, and ran down the stairs and into the food court under the terminal.

It was a busy Thursday afternoon and the lower level of the Kidapawan bus station was a jostling mass of hungry travellers, eager merchants and cheery musicians. The noise of the crowd filled the air and echoed off the concrete surrounds in jolly cacophony.

Gracia had barely had time to purchase her durian when the muffled noise of a bomb slammed into her young body. The food court around her dissolved into a frenzy of shock and dismay but it was above them, where the Weena buses were parked, that the desperate bloodshed unfolded.

The explosion took the lives of two passengers immediately, left six others fatally wounded, and dozens more injured. Around the bus where Gracia had lazed wearily, just minutes before, there now lay a tangled mess of ragged steel and bloodied victims.

Investigators would later determine that it was a homemade bomb, filled with nails and shredded iron in order to affect the greatest carnage. The device had been hidden in the Weena terminal, near the back of Gracia's parked bus. According to reports, it was an extortion attempt; a vicious demand by a local gang for the payment of 'protection money'.

But for Gracia, none of that mattered. For her, there remained only a peculiar sense of fate; of safeguarding and destiny. If not for the strange yearning that had overcome her as they arrived at the station, Gracia knew that she would have felt the full force of the blast. She would have joined the eight others who lost their lives that Thursday afternoon at the Kidapawan bus terminal.

Welcome to *Infinite Mind*. This book is a compilation of what I have learned about the capabilities of the human mind. It is by no means exhaustive, and (unlike the number 42) it does not offer concrete answers to life, the universe and everything.[2] It is simply a snapshot of our understanding of mystical phenomena in the early 21st century and the science that is beginning to unravel the mysteries of these natural experiences.

The anecdotes in this book are true. The characters in each chapter — whether historical or contemporary, famous or unfamiliar — are real. In most cases, the narratives detailed in this book have been recreated from personal memoirs, autobiographies or interviews, and the facts surrounding each event have been reproduced as accurately as possible.

It is tempting to label these events as 'remarkable' or 'extraordinary'. (In a world obsessed with sensationalism, it would certainly help with the marketing of this book!) However, to do so would compromise the integrity of these anecdotes and do a disservice to the scientists who have braved ridicule (and even poor funding) over the past hundred years to explore these phenomena.

The stories in this book are not as remarkable as they may appear — not as incredible. They are examples of some of the millions of intuitive insights, messages and inspirations that occur every year, all over the world.[3] These experiences, and the abilities associated with them, have come to be known by many names — psychic, metaphysical, paranormal, ESP, super natural — however I believe that many of these words are outdated and misleading. Therefore, throughout this book, I prefer to use the word psi, (pronounced sigh), when referring to these experiences.

Psi (Ψ) is the 23rd letter of the Greek alphabet and refers to anything 'of the soul'. In recent years, it has been adopted by scientists as the most appropriate term to describe the mental abilities that appear to sit outside our five, physical senses. Included in this umbrella term are telepathy, clairvoyance, precognition, psychokinesis and a host of other mental aptitudes that I will explain in detail in the coming chapters.

My use of the word psi is deliberate. Many psi researchers have adopted the term to avoid the use of misleading prefixes such as tele-, para- or extra-; prefixes that suggest attributes about these abilities that we now

believe to be incorrect. I use the term psi simply to avoid the
negative connotation that is associated with other terms that
are no longer useful; the unfortunate images of fortune
tellers, crystal balls and questionable 1900 hotlines that
inevitably spring to mind when confronted with words
such as psychic or ESP.

As science helps move us further from the
superstitions of the past, my hope is that these worn-out
phrases will also fade into oblivion. And it is indisputable
that science is moving us into exciting new territory.

Many scientific principles taught in schools today, in
the 21st century, are based on discoveries of the 17th and
18th centuries, particularly the philosophy of Rene
Descartes and the science of Isaac Newton. These early
discoverers introduced a way of thinking that explored the
workings of the universe yet did so without challenging the
strict doctrines of the powerful Church. As a result, their
findings were officially accepted by religious leaders and,
in turn, these 'acceptable' teachings became the standard for
future generations of scientists.

It is only in the last hundred years that flaws in these
principles have come to light. Modern psychology has, for
example, thrown into question Descartes' idea of the mind.
Experiments in quantum mechanics have revealed that
Newtonian physics does not always apply at a sub-atomic
level.

However, 400 years ago, science had taken a
decidedly materialistic turn and it was left to the mystics to
try to explain the thousands of ethereal and metaphysical

events experienced by people around the world. Over the centuries, certain concepts have arisen in an attempt to explain to those who had experienced unusual events — such as spirit guides, angels and demons — what science had chosen to ignore. We now understand that the conscious mind will interpret psi information in a way that is meaningful to the recipient. Although psi is believed to be the result of some form of pure 'data', an individual's prior beliefs and expectations will transform it into familiar imagery; for example, the angels of the Christian faith or the animal totems of indigenous Americans. Therefore, many mystical anecdotes (even those of the modern day) may involve such imagery.

Even early psi researchers misunderstood the nature of psi abilities, often working under the assumption that information collected was transferred by some form of radio wave or signal. Although understandable, based on the science of the time, sadly this misconception only contributed to the divide between science and spirituality as no such radio or thought signal was ever detected.

Thankfully, due largely to the evolution of quantum physics over the past century, new understandings are emerging about psi and how it fits into the human experience. Modern psi researchers maintain that psi phenomenon is a result of the interconnectedness of everything in the universe; a premise that is based on the discovery that the quantum universe is not a jigsaw of separate entities but rather an inescapable mass of intertwined energy and particles. The atoms that make up you and me do not stand apart from the atoms of our environment; they are intertwined, unified and in constant interaction. More on this in a later chapter.

The concepts of entanglement and non-locality (the ability of one particle to influence another distant particle without the transfer of information) have opened the door for modern psi researchers to create robust and testable theories about the nature of psi. Given this new understanding of the world, this quantum world, it seems entirely possible that information could be received across distance (and time) without any apparent transfer or signal.

Finally, after 400 years of deep division, the stage is set for psi to be explored and understood in scientific terms. It is this magical land, previously a no-man's-land, where scientific data meets spiritual lore that awaits you, dear reader, in the chapters that follow.

2

A Strange and Intense Dream
Seattle WA, USA

Jasmine's eyes flickered open and slowly adjusted to the early morning light. She stretched luxuriously and gently — the familiar surroundings of her bedroom came into focus and her dream fell away. She realised that she was exactly where she should be: in her student apartment in Seattle, Washington.

It had been such a strange and intense dream — the hospital room, her father standing next to her, the presence of her mother. She was sitting up in the hospital bed, cradling an infant baby in her arms. Lovingly, she had turned to look down into the eyes of the newborn child. The confusion of that moment was still palpable.

Jasmine was 23 — old enough to start a family — but university life was a fulltime commitment and she wasn't currently dating. Even in her dream, she questioned this fact. She had no recollection of a pregnancy and no concept of who the father might be. *Who is this baby? Where did it come from? When was I pregnant?* Nothing in the dream made sense. For this reason, it should be dismissed as inconsequential — the random imaginings of a nocturnal mind. But something about the dream hung on her like a thick blanket of significance. She could not shake the puzzling visions it had brought her.

Thanks to her American father and Malaysian mother, Jasmine had olive skin, brown wavy hair and eyes the colour of melted chocolate. She had always assumed that her children would share these physical traits, so she had been startled by the baby in her dream. It was a boy with blonde hair, blue eyes and the fairest of skin. It was a Western European baby and Jasmine remembered referring to it, in her dream, as a little Frenchman.

Despite the initial confusion, Jasmine's connection with the tiny baby in her dream had been deep and profound, and this sat with her as she lay in bed in the early Seattle sunlight. Deep inside, she knew this was not just any baby. This was *her* baby; her little Frenchman.

The feeling did not leave her all day. Raised to be logical and pragmatic, Jasmine tried repeatedly throughout the day to shrug the dream off as an irrational illusion, but in vain. Finally, she accepted that somehow, in her sleep, a tiny blue-eyed infant had wrapped himself around her heart. When her phone rang that evening, it was a welcome distraction.

Darain was an old friend from high school. A year older than Jasmine, Darain had watched over her throughout their teenage years in Honolulu — like a protective older brother. He had left Hawaii several years earlier to attend the Coast Guard Academy in Connecticut, and it was only by chance that they had both ended up in

Seattle — Jasmine studying nursing at the University of Washington, and Darain with his first duty station with the Coast Guard.

Jasmine was pleased to hear his voice and was even more delighted when he suggested a night out later in the week. Darain explained that his brother, Robin, was in town and it was a perfect opportunity for the three high school buddies to have a fun reunion. Jasmine's eerie dream was forgotten, and she glided through the week in a pleasant and comfortable routine.

From the moment Darain picked her up, they were absorbed in conversation. He explained that he had invited a couple of extra friends, but Jasmine barely registered this as she slipped into the front of the car and continued their lively dialogue. The laughter, banter and gossip continued into the restaurant.

Darain sat opposite Jasmine, and Robin, keen to hear her news, sat beside her. As they took their places, Jasmine glanced further down the table realising that she was yet to acknowledge the other guests. Her gaze flickered past the first companion, a Coast Guard friend of Darain's, and came to rest lightly on the second stranger.

He had not yet uttered a word, in fact he was still settling into his seat, but the message in Jasmine's mind was immediate and emphatic. *This man is going to be in your life, for the rest of your life.* Jasmine looked away swiftly, struggling to find a rational reason for such a bizarre thought. It was a few moments before she turned back to look at the stranger at the opposite end of the table.

In that instant, her body froze. There, looking back at her, were the familiar features and cornflour blue eyes of the baby in her dream.

His name was Kevin. Originally from the East Coast, he had just received his commission into the Coast Guard and had been stationed to a boat in Seattle. Darain had taken Kevin under his wing, and was keeping him company while he assimilated to his new life on the West Coast.

Kevin was quiet that evening. He watched as the three friends engaged in enthusiastic and nostalgic conversation, interjecting only occasionally to offer a witty or humorous remark. But for Jasmine, the connection was immediate and intimate. Despite the protests of her logical mind, the quiet stranger at the end of the table felt like he was already part of her family. She felt like she already knew Kevin, and she was keen to investigate why.

The next day, she contacted Darain. "Who is Kevin? Where do I know him from?"

Darain's reply was both intriguing and revealing. "There's no way you would know him," he said. "His name is Kevin Beaudoin. He's from Massachusetts, but he's half French."

A week later, thanks to Darain, Kevin and Jasmine met again, this time at Jasmine's apartment. It was only a brief visit, but it served to reinforce the feeling within Jasmine that Kevin was to be part of her life. That evening, after the two men had left, Jasmine's roommate watched her running through the apartment gleefully yelling "I'm going to marry that man!" Her prediction proved to be correct.

After a year abroad with the Coast Guard, Kevin returned to Seattle to enjoy his first official date with Jasmine, and they were married less than two years later. They currently have two daughters — one is blonde with cornflour blue eyes.

Psi in dreams: Sidestepping the senses

According to researchers, psi-related dreams (dreams that include telepathic, clairvoyant or precognitive information) are the most common form of psi experience. In fact, studies from around the world show that about half of all spontaneous psi experiences happen while the recipient is dreaming, and most include a subject of great emotional impact or importance.[4]

In 1966, in response to a growing volume of anecdotal evidence, psychiatrist Montague Ullman began a series of clinical tests at the Maimonides dream laboratory in Brooklyn, New York. Over the next seven years, Ullman and his colleagues completed a total of 379 dream-psi sessions and produced some of the most compelling evidence for psi ever collected.

The success of dream-psi experiments, and the regularity with which prophetic dreams appear in the wider population, suggests that psi is fundamentally an unconscious process. As a result, it seems to be naturally heightened once the distraction of the five physical senses has been removed or neutralised. On a cultural level, this may explain the use of altered states of awareness by traditional shamans — such as meditation, drumming and psychoactive drugs — when attempting to receive intuitive insights and messages.

According to researchers, precognitive dreams (like the one Jasmine had) tend to be exceptionally poignant and clear, and often contain unusual or bizarre information. Although many of these dreams carry a sense of significance, it can initially be difficult to identify them as precognitive or symbolic. However, because psi-related dreams are relatively common, it is possible for anyone to learn to identify them as they occur.

The first step in identifying psi-related dreams is to learn how to identify normal (non-psi) dreams. Non-psi dreams are:

1. generic; a dream influenced by the previous day's activities and thoughts, or
2. wish-fulfilling; a dream of a desire or aspiration, or
3. anxiety-disclosing; a dream which reveals an unconscious (or conscious) fear or concern.

Dreams that feel significant, that are full of unusual content and do not represent any of the above categories, may be psi-based. Often, these dreams involve precognitive or telepathic messages; psi information that is bypassing your conscious mind, while you sleep.

3

A Silent Force
Pretoria, South Africa

The young Englishman stood motionless and waited, his heart beating wildly. In the darkness, the arguing voices drew closer.

He held his breath and pressed his slender body further against the side of the carriage, pleading for the night to render him invisible. The voices were mainly African, but occasionally among the deep unmodulated tones of the Africans, a more sinister guttural European tongue was barking commands. There was a Boer with them.

Swiftly, all hopes of boarding the train unseen were abandoned. Despairing, the young man turned from the carriage and willed his tired body forward. Adjusting his eyes to the night, he slipped off the tracks and back onto the limitless plains of the Highveld.

It was over 48 hours since his escape from the prisoner of war camp in Pretoria. What was left of his chocolate — his only source of food — had melted beyond recognition in the sweltering December heat. As darkness folded around him, the young man's thoughts turned to survival.

Although trained in the military, his passion was journalism and he had come to South Africa as a War Correspondent. In search of a story, he joined a reconnaissance trip in Natal, on board an armoured train. It was an ill-fated decision; the train was ambushed by the Boers, and he was captured in the gun fight that followed. He tried for weeks to secure his release — arguing that he was a civilian — but the Boer authorities had not been sympathetic and his patience had run dry. Finally, in a moment of boldness, he had scaled the walls of the State Models School camp and set out for the Portuguese port of Delagoa Bay, 300 miles to the east.

As he trudged wearily into the darkness he noticed, to his left, a faint glimmer of light that signalled the presence of an African kraal. It occurred to our young man that beside those flickering flames he might find a warm meal and a bed for the night. It was also well known that the local Africans had no love for the Boers. *At the very least*, he thought, *I won't be arrested*. The thought of another night without food spurred him on, and he stumbled toward the kraal.

A mile into the journey, his footsteps halted abruptly and he was overcome with doubt. Many Blacks were spies for the Boers, and he could not be sure that his English currency would buy their allegiance. He turned and headed back to the railway line.

Less than half the distance back to the tracks, he paused again. The trains offered no safety for him. Even, if by some miracle, he could identify an east-bound train, he was almost certain to be recaptured or, he shuddered at the thought, killed by some over-zealous Boer. In an instant, the hopelessness of his situation crystallised in his mind. Despair took hold of him and the young man sank to his knees in the boggy soil. Exhausted, he rested his heavy head in his hands and surrendered his fate to the vast South African wilderness.

The feeling came suddenly, flowing gently out of the darkness and embracing him like a warm blanket of reassurance. A wave of quiet knowing washed over him and all traces of doubt dissolved. Consumed with a bold certainty, his body urged him to act without delay. As unexpected as the sensation was, it was not entirely foreign to him. It was similar to the intuitive certainty that he had experienced many times before in the world of séances and mystics. With newfound conviction, the young man set off towards the distant glow of the kraal.

The lights were further away than he anticipated, and it was many hours before he realised that he was not heading towards the hearth fires of an African kraal. Instead, he found himself at a coalmine, the flames of the furnaces glowing brightly in the night sky. Around the mouth of the mine, a cluster of low buildings crouched in the darkness.

The 'knowing' deep inside our young man had not abated, and he approached a large stone house and knocked loudly on the door. It was answered promptly by the coalmine manager, who did not seem too perturbed by the rude awakening in the middle of the night. Instead, he ushered the weary traveller inside and listened as the young man with a crisp accent and a lisp told his story.

As the tale finished, the traveller eyed his host carefully, searching for signs of hostility or menace. After a long pause, the miner rose slowly to his feet and quietly locked the door. The young man steeled himself for certain recapture.

His fears were unfounded. Suddenly, without warning, the miner turned and stretched out his hand in a warm greeting. "Thank God you have come here!" he exclaimed. "It is the only house for twenty miles where you would not be handed over. But we are all British here and we will see you through."

Relieved and bewildered the young man returned the handshake, and thanked the silent force that had led him to safety; that interminable knowing that had saved his life, and would return to do so many times in his illustrious future.

"My name is John Howard," the miner offered warmly. "Never mind, we'll fix you up somehow."

"I'm grateful for your help, Mr Howard," the young man replied. "My name is Winston. Winston Churchill."

In 1900, after being smuggled by John Howard into Portuguese territory, Winston Churchill returned to England as a hero and later became the one of the greatest wartime leaders the world has ever seen. On at least two occasions during World War II, Churchill's uncanny intuition saved his life and the lives of others, and he remained an active supporter of the mystical movement in England until his death in 1965.

Claircognizance: The awareness of knowing

Claircognizance literally means 'clear understanding' or 'clear knowledge'. This word is sometimes used to describe the ability to receive psi knowledge or understanding by means of a thought, idea or creative inspiration.

In recent years, several scientific theories have arisen to support the idea that we are all connected at a quantum level. And some researchers have provided evidence that we are all able to draw upon data and knowledge that lies beyond our sphere of personal experience and awareness. For instance, biologist Rupert Sheldrake has demonstrated *morphic resonance*, a phenomenon whereby animals can share new knowledge and information globally, without any apparent form of communication.[5]

What these new theories propose is that, at a deep level, we have an unlimited amount of knowledge available to us at any given time. It follows that a claircognizant event — such as the one Winston Churchill experienced in December 1899 — occurs, not because we obtain new knowledge, but because we become aware of knowledge that we already possess.

Claircognizance can manifest in the following ways:

- Certainty about a situation — an overwhelming sense of knowing
- Recalling information you cannot remember learning, or could not have learned
- Sudden ideas, inventions or solutions popping into your head — often in their entirety.

4

Quiet Epiphany
Kittyhawk, Apollo 14

Edgar could finally relax. After six days of intense focus all was quiet in the Kittyhawk, and all was well.

Outside the capsule, kept at bay by a few inches of aluminium alloy, the vast vacuum of space stretched on into infinity. Behind them Fra Mauro, the lunar landing site, was slowly falling away into the distance and onto the pages of history books throughout the world.

Around him, the bustling efficiency of the day had been replaced by a reverent stillness. Edgar glanced at his sleeping comrades and allowed himself a deep, satisfied sigh. He had performed everything NASA had required of him — his scientific efforts on the moon had been described as "excellent" — and he was now, finally, on his way home. Edgar let the weightless embrace of space take hold of him as he drifted off into a delicate sleep.

It had been a long road for Edgar Mitchell, the farm boy from western Texas. From the prairies of the south-west, Edgar's journey had taken him through the scientific laboratories of university and into the cockpits of the US

Navy flight squadron. Throughout these years, it was not his intellect that had stood him apart from his peers, (although he was a competent and serious student). What Edgar possessed was an insatiable quest for knowledge; a burning desire to see how far human understanding, and human technology, could be expanded.

Edgar's curiosity knew no limits. Although raised as a Southern Baptist, his pursuit of knowledge ran far beyond religious dogma or traditional doctrines. He shunned ignorance, abhorred apathy and ignored all limitations. Edgar was an explorer of the mind and of human capability — constantly striving to be at the forefront of ingenuity. So, when the Soviets launched Sputnik in 1957, Edgar sensed that manned space flight was within reach and he knew he had to be a part of it.

For the next nine years, Edgar travelled all over the United States pursuing his single-minded dream of becoming a space pioneer. He studied Aeronautic Engineering in California, completed a doctorate in Aeronautics and Astronautics in Massachusetts and became a test pilot in Arizona under the direction of the incomparable Chuck Yeager. Finally, in 1966, the call came from NASA and Edgar was invited to join the fledgling US space program.

Three years later, safely confined in six cubic metres of NASA spacecraft, Edgar's inherent craving for exploration had ultimately taken him beyond any earthly limits. At 41 years old, he had escaped the confines of the

Earth's atmosphere, walked proudly on the moon and glimpsed the eternity of the universe. What had been a life-long intellectual journey was quickly transformed into something more profound, more sacred, than Edgar could ever imagine.

The Kittyhawk was a well-functioning craft. The minor glitches that had plagued the crew in the early days of the mission had all but disappeared, and Edgar's role as Systems Engineer was pleasantly undemanding. Radio contact with Houston was routine and relaxed, and the crew were only interrupted occasionally for cheerful interviews with the press. As the Lunar Module Pilot and Mission Scientist, the lion's share of Edgar's work had been conducted on the Moon's surface and in the delicate few hours the lunar lander was in flight. Now, with the moon behind them and the lunar module safely docked with the command module, Edgar had little to do except bask in a state of relaxed satisfaction. For the first time on the mission, he was free to contemplate the incredible vista that lay beyond the five, small windows of the command module.

The Kittyhawk was designed to roll gently as it hurtled through space, completing one rotation every two minutes. Inside the spacecraft, Edgar became increasingly mesmerised by the shifting outlook that this provided. Earth, moon, sun and a multitude of stars and galaxies; each passed before his eyes in a never-ending, cyclical panorama. Without the interference of light pollution or atmosphere, the view of space took on a new level of intensity and magnificence. The stars were 10 times brighter and more numerous than anywhere on Earth and the planet itself was wrapped in a peaceful aura of shimmering light.

As he lay in the Kittyhawk, quietly absorbing the view, an overwhelming sense of awe and wonder began to form inside Edgar. His insatiable inner-explorer came to life and he began to ponder the scientific implications of what he was seeing.

It occurred to him how little humans know of themselves and the universe and he realised that, if humanity is to venture into the cool unknown of space, it was vital to expand this understanding.

He saw the tiny planet that was Earth — his home. He watched the moon — the great human conquest of the twentieth century, and the sun — a life-giving miracle, a nuclear reactor of unimaginable magnitude. He saw the stars in their magnificent intensity and realised that everything he had ever seen, everything he had ever been, had come from the discarded atoms of stars, billions of years ago. The spacecraft, his comrades beside him and the planet that was slowly drawing nearer all were made of nothing but stardust.

With each new thought, Edgar's awareness opened and expanded and his body flowed with joyous understanding. Lost in his quiet epiphany, Edgar realised that he did not stand apart from the universe, he was *one with it*. His atoms were the atoms of the stars, his mind was a tiny fragment of a grand intelligence and his life was an integral part of a complex and miraculous process.

Edgar bathed in the awesome fullness of this knowledge and was consumed with the bliss of enlightenment. However, he was not overcome by the presence of an external being. This was not a mystical or religious experience. Nor was he transported to another reality. Instead, he could feel his mind reorganising itself to accommodate this new information. He could sense his ingrained perceptions and prejudices dissolving to incorporate the truth of what he was seeing. For Edgar, this was an enlightening journey of the mind, an exploration of consciousness.

Over the next few days, as the Earth grew larger in the capsule windows, Edgar's sense of ecstasy and unity continued. And, by the time the Kittyhawk burst through the Earth's fragile atmosphere, he was convinced that his sense of oneness with the universe was not based in mysticism or superstition. He had glimpsed a reality that earthly sciences, and most human minds, were yet to discover.

On 9 February 1971, nine days, one minute and 20 seconds after launch, the NASA Apollo 14 mission splashed down in the South Pacific Ocean. On board were astronauts Alan Shepard, Stuart Roosa and Edgar Mitchell.

Almost immediately after the mission, Edgar began intensive research into the enlightenment that had overwhelmed him on his trip home (and that returned many times afterwards, often while in an aircraft). He soon discovered that many ancient cultures referenced this occurrence. For instance, *Samadhi* which is contained in the ancient Sanskrit writings of India, is described as the state of recognising everything as being separate, whilst understanding this separateness is just an illusion. This discovery strengthened Edgar's conviction that his epiphany was a natural part of the human experience.

In 1972, Edgar left NASA and founded the Institute of Noetic Sciences, a not-for-profit organisation that supports the scientific research of consciousness, psi and human potential. For over 40 years, until his death in February 2016, he remained an avid supporter of scientific and technological exploration, and continued to challenge the self-imposed limits of human understanding.

Global consciousness: The entangled universe

One of the most pervasive ideas of our time is that we are all made of solid 'stuff' — each separate and apart from the 'stuff' that sits alongside us. I am *here*, and you are *there*. In order to affect each other there must be some form of communication or movement from *here* to *there*. Furthermore, nothing can move between *here* and *there* faster than the speed of light.

It is this premise that underpins most traditional science and, arguably, our entire perspective of reality.

However, discoveries at the quantum level have turned this notion on its head and have begun to disassemble the material universe as we know it. Thanks to recent discoveries in quantum physics, it is now widely understood that the building blocks of matter — even the most solid materials — are not solid at all. In fact, at a sub-atomic level, matter does not appear to resemble matter, but rather an almost incomprehensible mass of probability, interaction and curious space-time relationships.

For instance, it is now accepted that a light photon can be both a particle and a wave *at the same time*.[6] It is also possible for an atom to be in two places, and/or spin in opposite directions, simultaneously.

Interestingly, evidence has also emerged that objects up to the size of small diamonds can remain linked across distance and time and can display instant, correlative behaviour without any traditional form of communication or interaction.[7] The discovery of this concept spawned the terms *entanglement* and *non-locality* — although Einstein, aware of this behaviour, famously referred to it as "spooky action at a distance".

Entanglement refers to the linking or entwining of objects, and non-locality describes the correlated behaviour of entangled objects across distance and/or time. It is worth reiterating that neither of these concepts are fantastical ideas nor far-fetched theories; they are part of a new scientific reality and have been demonstrated with increasing frequency and reliability since the turn of the new millennium.

If we are to assume that the Big Bang theory holds some validity (and all matter in the universe was once concentrated into one, single particle) then it can be surmised that every object of this universe has the potential to be entangled with every other object. And, moreover, these objects may be instantaneously connecting with and behaving in accordance with other objects throughout the universe.

Put simply, every atom of your body may realistically have an inherent connection to every other part of this universe. Just as Dr Edgar Mitchell came to realise during his return to Earth in 1971, the long-held assumption that objects are distinct and separate from each other no longer stands up to scrutiny. The new scientific reality is that you do not exist apart from the universe. In fact, you are inextricably connected with it and, potentially, constantly interacting with it. You are *one with* the universe.

Although entanglement occurs at a sub-atomic level, there is a growing understanding that quantum processes have very real repercussions on a macro level — the level we perceive with our senses. One of the most compelling studies to provide evidence of interconnectedness on a real-world scale is the Global Consciousness Project (GCP).

Since it was launched at Princeton University in 1998, the GCP has gathered remarkable statistical evidence of a correlation between human attention and the behaviour of Random Number Generators (RNGs) placed in various locations around the world. According to the collected data, there is an almost undeniable effect on the physical world (the RNGs) whenever a large mass of people is focused on the same event. The more dramatic the event (September 11 terror attacks; the opening of the Olympic Games), the more the RNGs are affected by an unseen force. After 15 years of serious study and more than 450 tests, it has become apparent that even our thoughts and emotions are somehow entwined with, and can affect, the physical universe.

It is this new reality of interconnectedness and unity that is breaking down old preconceptions about the universe we live in, and opening the doorway for a deeper understanding of how psi phenomena work.

5

The Clear and Insistent Thought
Little Rock AR, USA

Edwina fumbled with the deadbolt, entered the darkened apartment and closed the door against the warm night air. It had been a busy shift on the ward, and she was determined to reward herself with a sip of cold beer and a cigarette.

It was 18 months since she had moved from small-town New Zealand to Little Rock, Arkansas and the culture shock had finally numbed to a dull indifference. She no longer suffered unbearably in the summer heat, or felt awkwardly conspicuous among her African-American neighbours. Even the nightly gunfire from local gang fights, a sound completely foreign to her in her homeland, had eventually faded into the tapestry of familiar background noise.

Her friends had been horrified when she decided to move to the "South Side", but Edwina loved her apartment and thrived in the eclectic buzz of her working class neighbourhood. Although basic, her complex was always tidy, the gardens and pool were well maintained and she was sure that the drug dealer downstairs kept a protective eye on her.

Her second storey apartment was compact but airy — the living area had a large, low window which filled the space with daylight. In keeping with the neighbourhood, the apartment was simply furnished. It was only in the bedroom that she had allowed herself one indulgence — a large bed with beautiful, carefully selected linen.

It was to this humble home that Edwina returned every night, after the evening shift.

Her work as a registered nurse at the local children's hospital was simultaneously rewarding and exhausting. As soon as she arrived home, Edwina would switch the television on to MTV, clean off her makeup, don fresh pyjamas and settle on the couch for a cold beer, a cigarette and a late night movie. Her nights had a comfortable and relaxing routine.

This evening felt no different, and not even Edwina realised when her steps diverted from their usual pattern. Tonight, her fresh pyjamas lay unused; her makeup remained on her young face. Instead, with MTV blaring and still in her nursing scrubs, Edwina walked to the kitchen and reached for a can of beer in the fridge. She returned to the living room, and settled on the couch that took pride of place in front of the window. From here, she'd normally be able to see down into the pool area but the curtains had been drawn before she had left for work, and it was the television that took her attention. She opened the can, took a long sip of beer and reached for a cigarette.

Suddenly, Edwina hesitated. Her hand remained still, hovering over the cigarette packet as if held by an intense magnetism. From the back of her head came the clear and insistent thought, *You have to go to bed, right now,* and like a well-trained soldier, her body swiftly and automatically obeyed.

The cigarettes lay untouched; the full can of beer was forgotten. Edwina reached for the remote, turned off the television and the lights and walked to her bed.

Within seconds, gunshots rang out. Five, then one more.

As she changed into her pyjamas and pulled the luxurious bed sheets over her, Edwina thought how close the gunshots had sounded. Then she gently drifted off to sleep.

It was close to nine in the morning when Edwina awoke. Her makeup was still on from the night before and felt oily and clogged. Bleary-eyed, she stumbled out of her bedroom and stopped in horror at the scene before her.

Inside the living room, the floor was covered in plaster from the cheap plasterboard lining her apartment, and her couch glittered with a dusting of shattered glass. The closed curtains were strangely askew and they swayed in the breeze coming through the broken window.

Edwina turned to look at the wall against which she had sat hours before. There, embedded in the plaster were the scorched ends of six bullets.

It was never determined if the bullets were meant for Edwina, or if they were simply the result of an all-too-close gang fight, but one fact remained: if Edwina had not listened to the internal voice that ordered her off the couch and out of harm's way, the bullets now implanted in the wall would have peppered her body.

Edwina left her apartment that morning and never returned. Nine days later, she boarded a plane for a new life in London, abandoning her home, her furniture and her beloved luxury linen without so much as a backwards glance. She now lives in Perth, Australia where she runs a luxury menswear company.

Clairaudience: the voice of wisdom

Clairaudience literally means 'clear hearing'. The term is sometimes used to describe the experience of receiving psi knowledge or information as an audible thought, or some other form of audible information.

Contrary to popular superstition, clairaudient information is not usually an external voice in the recipient's ear. Instead, the information tends to manifest as profound and clear words, amplified inside the recipient's head in their 'inner-monologue' voice (as it was with Edwina). Clairaudience may also cause the recipient to focus upon a particular sound in the immediate environment, for instance the words of a song, or a nearby conversation.

Throughout human history there have been mentions of clairaudient experiences. They have often compelled the actions of prophets, philosophers and revolutionaries. Of special note is Greek philosopher Socrates, who openly attributed his philosophical genius to his daemon — a voice that spoke only to him. "You have heard me say often and in many places that a voice is present with me ... Now this began with me from my childhood; a certain voice, which always, when it comes, turns me aside from that which I am about to do, but never impels me to do anything."[8]

Although fairly common, clairaudient information can be difficult to detect as it tends to be overshadowed by everyday thoughts. Initially, this information is most likely to be recognised during times of stillness or meditation, or when the information is delivered in an emphatic manner, as with the case of Edwina.

6

Buckle In Tight
Middlesex, UK

The chilly November air gnawed at Hannah's fingers as she unlocked her Ford Fiesta. Hastily, she opened the door, slipped behind the wheel and rubbed her frosty hands together until the numbness subsided. Then, she placed the key in the ignition.

Be careful!

Hannah barely registered the now-familiar warning. The voice had been with her for the past few weeks and she had become accustomed to its presence. Now, with a quick flick of her hand, she swatted the message at its apparent source — several inches from her head, in the air above her right shoulder.

Hannah had often heard voices as a young child but, at the insistence of her father, she'd learned to lock them out. "When the voices come, you just shut your eyes and tell them to go away," he had said. So, she had. From the age of four, Hannah's voices had ceased to exist and their presence had dimmed with time into a collection of vague childhood memories. Until now.

The voice that spoke to her now was male — strong and insistent — but there was no menace in the message it delivered. *Be careful!* — the same protective voice prompted her, urged her, every time she got into a car. The experience was ongoing and unusual enough for Hannah to have mentioned it to a friend. But she didn't attach a lot of meaning to the mysterious message. She was 18, healthy and vibrant. To Hannah, the unshakable optimist, there seemed little reason to be any more vigilant than usual.

Hannah checked her reflection in the rear-vision mirror, slotted a tape into the cassette player and put the car into gear. Life was good and Hannah smiled softly to herself as she headed out into the hectic morning traffic.

******

The weeks rolled on and by 8 December 1989, a wintery pall had settled over Stanwell, Middlesex. For most of the day, low cloud and a light drizzle had blocked the sun and muffled the constant noise of the jets flowing through nearby Heathrow Airport. But it was Friday and Hannah was in a buoyant mood.

By mid-afternoon, the weather had brightened to match Hannah's optimism and the sun greeted her as she left the office. It was the weekend; she was free. Tonight, with her closest friends, Hannah would be celebrating the simple joy of being young and alive. It was a weekly celebration, and one that she relished.

Hannah's boyfriend, Steve, was a well-respected floor layer with a solid and reliable nature. He was a year older than Hannah; they had met through a mutual friend and had been dating for the past 18 months. She loved him for his quiet dependability; he loved her for her unconventional effervescence.

The third member of the trio was Dawn — quiet, refined, cautious Dawn. She and Hannah had shared classes at high school, but in the last couple of years they had grown extremely close. In many ways, they were polar opposites. Hannah was petite, blonde and bubbly, desperate for her independence. Dawn was tall, brunette and ravishingly beautiful — so much so that she was considering a career as a full-time model. To onlookers Hannah and Dawn made an unlikely pair. To each other they were best buddies — inseparable.

On occasion, the trio would head to the Hammersmith Palais, 14 miles to the east, but tonight the location was more local. This evening they were heading to The Angel, a pub in Staines-Upon-Thames.

Just before 8pm, Steve and Hannah climbed into Steve's Astra GT and headed to Dawn's house in nearby Bedfont. Around them, the streets were gleaming with the headlamps of the bustling traffic and above them the sky was littered with circling aircraft during the Friday rush at Heathrow. The air was crisp and cool, and Hannah was beaming with joy.

It took less than 10 minutes to drive the two miles from Stanwell to Bedfont, and Dawn was ready when they arrived. The girls had a lot to talk about — Dawn had a new boyfriend and her brother was soon to be married. The chatter started immediately as Hannah sprang from the two-door Astra and pulled her seat forward to let Dawn clamber into the back. Hannah was almost oblivious when she climbed into the passenger seat and a voice (familiar to her from the past few weeks) spoke loudly in her right ear: *Put your seatbelt on.*

It was not something she always did. Compulsory seatbelts had only been passed into law a few years prior, and then only for the front seat. Through a mixture of unconcern, forgetfulness and simmering teenage defiance, Hannah had often ignored the supposed safety of the seatbelt. But tonight, there was no conscious thought. The voice had spoken and, although she was lost in the enthusiasm of her best friend's chatter, her body simply obeyed. Immediately and automatically, Hannah pulled the strap across her chest and clicked the buckle in tight.

The plan was simple; drive back to Hannah's house where her parents would shuttle them to The Angel. So, no drinking and driving; everybody would be safe.

The two girls continued their lively banter as Steve headed towards Stanwell. Dawn, all slender limbs and long hair, leaning forward out of the cramped back seat and Hannah twisted in her seat to chat back to her. A few minutes into their journey, Hannah turned just in time to see the lorry approaching from the other side of the intersection. "Watch out for that truck!" ....

Then blackness.

Hannah regained consciousness almost instantly with the impact of the crash consuming her senses. Hannah's eyes felt heavy as they focused on the smashed windscreen, her body was vibrating with the ferocious noise of the crash. She could taste crushed metal. Dazed and disorientated, she was aware of one thing only — the voice in her head commanding in a never-ending loop, *Get out of the car. Get out of the car. Get out of the car.* This was not a man's voice, this was her own voice, and her only desire was to obey it.

The impact of the crash had thrown Dawn forward into the windscreen and then back, into a tangled mess of hair and limbs, onto the back seat. Hannah was twisted at an uncomfortable angle against the passenger door and much of the front of the car was crushed under the chassis of the truck.

Hannah groped blindly to release her seatbelt. Dawn's hand, warm and limp, lay on top of the latch and as Hannah removed it she realised, in the far recesses of her brain, that the hand was lifeless. Her beloved friend was dead.

As she freed herself from the seatbelt, Hannah saw Steve. His blood-stained head, yellow liquid oozing from his ears, lay motionless on the gear stick. But she had no time to consider the implications, as a collection of anxious faces appeared at her window and began to crowbar her to safety.

Within minutes, Hannah was walking free. Her seatbelt, and the voice that had commanded that she use it, had saved her life. Behind her, in the mangled remains of

Steve's car, lay the motionless bodies of her two dearest friends.

Steve lay in a coma for the next two months but eventually awoke to begin the long road to rehabilitation. Emergency workers worked on Dawn for over an hour at the scene of the accident, but all efforts to revive her were unsuccessful.

Hannah's seatbelt ensured her physical body remained intact. Local police officers regarded it as a miracle survival and she walked away from the accident with nothing more than a slight tear where an earring was ripped from her earlobe. But the emotional scars are still evident in Hannah today, over 20 years on.

In the years since the tragedy, the male voice that spoke to Hannah has returned twice; each time to inform her of the death of a beloved grandparent. Hannah now lives in Sydney, Australia and has learned to regain her suppressed psi abilities — the abilities that came naturally to her when she was very young.

Intuitive children: unrestrained psi

In the mid-1970s Israeli psychic, Uri Geller, made a number of television appearances where he demonstrated his ability to bend spoons using just his mind (psychokinesis). After each appearance Dr Edgar Mitchell, who had worked closely with Uri, would receive frantic phone calls from parents whose children were unexpectedly emulating Geller's feat at the dining room table.[9]

From the late 1950s, psychologist Dr Ian Stevenson travelled the world researching young children who were spontaneously sharing details about their 'previous lives'. In 40 years, Dr Stevenson documented over 2000 cases, many of which were completely verified by matching deceased people with details provided by these children.[10]

Around the world, for thousands of years, parents have shared anecdotal details of their children seeing visions, having premonitions and speaking to deceased relatives.

But, how do these experiences fit into our modern understanding of psi? Are young children more aware of psi information, or do they simply have more vivid imaginations?

Over the last 20 years, psychologists have unlocked astonishing new understandings about the human brain and how it develops in infancy and childhood. In the early part of the twentieth century, it was assumed that a child's brain was a 'blank slate' and that life would write its stories as the child developed.

But recent studies show a young human brain is far more capable than previously thought. It is now suggested that during our early years our brains are wired to experience *anything* and *everything*. Rather than adding information to an empty database it seems that, as young children, we have the potential for a full range of experiences. We simply learn, over time, to disregard information or experience that is not vital to our individual circumstances.

Researcher Dr Patricia Kuhl has produced evidence to show that a human baby is capable of discerning any sound from any language around the world.[11] As the child grows older and begins to register the sounds that are required for their individual language, they lose the ability to discriminate the sounds of *other* languages. (Those sounds are not required for the child's individual circumstances therefore the brain considers them unimportant).

This evidence suggests that young children are naturally wired to have a *full* and *indiscriminate* experience of the world. Presumably, this full experience would also include the indiscriminate use of psi abilities; abilities that studies have shown to be inherent and widespread in the human population. It is feasible, then, that many young children experience psi phenomena simply because they have not yet been told it is impossible or unacceptable to do so.

Throughout history many parents have been openly fearful or sceptical of any form of psychic ability. Therefore, it is probable that most children, particularly in the West, have learned to block out or disregard any psi information they receive. As with Hannah, who was encouraged to ignore her voices by her father, natural psi experiences may be disregarded by the developing brain as unwanted or unnecessary. Researchers are discovering that once our beliefs and paradigms have been established, it is very difficult for us to experience (or acknowledge) anything that is not part of our expected reality.[12]

Psychologist Daniel Simons is well known for his studies into "inattentional blindness". Dr Simon's experiment, humorously nick-named *Gorillas in the midst*, involved a video of a group of people passing around a basketball. People are asked to watch the video and count the passes. While the ball is being passed from person to person, a gorilla unexpectedly appears in the video behind them. Overwhelmingly, people watching the video were completely unaware of the gorilla casually walking into the shot and thumping its chest proudly. The gorilla is not expected, nor is it necessary to the task, so the adult brain does not perceive it.

When dealing with psi in youngsters it is worth remembering that young children experience the world *as it is*, whereas adults perceive the world as they *expect it to be*. Psychic experience is a natural part of many children's lives and, as psi becomes more accepted, it is reasonable to expect that more and more people will carry these abilities through into adulthood.

7

To Be an Artist
Hay NSW, Australia

1952

Kevin's world is ochre and olive. At 11 years old, he has only ever experienced Hay; a sleepy town in the featureless south-west corner of New South Wales, Australia. His is a world of limited colours — of gold and orange; of grey-green and beige — as if Mother Nature had only used part of the palette when she made her long, even brushstrokes across the landscape. The only deviation from this colour scheme was the sky; a vast, curving canvas of sapphire blue that had been placed, as if as an afterthought, above the sun-kissed plains.

It was this Outback landscape — flat, expansive and fiery — that Kevin understood and adored. It was all he had ever known. Which is why his dream was so intriguing.

The vision had come to him several times over the past year and the memory of it had embedded itself in his childhood mind. It was a static dream; a still-life image of a world Kevin could never have imagined.

Each time the dream comes, it is the same. He is no longer in the vastness of the Outback but in an urban setting, surrounded by innumerable buildings. He is standing on a road, sleek with bitumen. In front of him is an immense sandstone wall — a solid mass of yellow, pink and taupe that lords over its surroundings and threatens to block out every inch of sky.

Fingers of ivy flow over the top of the wall and spill toward the ground in rivulets of dark green. Over the wall, Kevin can glimpse the russet tiles of a large, impressive rooftop; a jumble of angles, eaves and intersections. At the roadside, the expanse of sandstone is broken only by a nondescript wrought iron gate, set low against the footpath. On the left of the gate, sits an unusual metal box which seems to stare, defiantly at Kevin.

The image holds no meaning to Kevin but the vision had become a regular night-time ritual; a familiar snapshot of an unknown place and time.

*****

1967

Even the sinister flamboyance of Kings Cross — usually a brash and defiant Sydney suburb — had been dulled to a silvery grey. Clouds hung low and heavy overhead and the rain pelted a syncopated rhythm on the taxi roof, as the *whoomp, whoomp, whoomp* of the windshield wipers kept time.

I am an artist. Kevin was still uncomfortable with the idea, like a designer coat he was yet to grow into. But today, more than ever, he needed it to be true.

It was less than a year since he had left the town of Shepparton to pursue his dream in Sydney. The notion sounded romantic — honourable even — but the raw truth was that life in Shepparton had become intolerable. As the manager of a local restaurant (tearooms by day; youthful hangout by night) Kevin had witnessed his fair share of thuggery, illicit deals and unsavoury behaviour. After 6pm, when the pubs were closed, it was to Kevin's establishment the stumbling, bleary-eyed hordes would come, restless for entertainment, folk-rock music and trouble.

In an era of strict alcohol laws and free-spirited youth, maintaining order each night took a heavy toll on Kevin. Eventually, it was the actions of a silver-spooned young hoodlum and his belligerent attempt to smuggle alcohol onto the premises that had pushed the pendulum too far. With the takings of his last night — a meagre $80 — Kevin had turned his back on life in regional Australia and decided to try his luck in Sydney. He was going to be an artist.

His first night in the big city had shown little promise. He had slept in a park until the police told him to move on.

It took a couple of days for Kevin to secure himself a bed in Kings Cross. A few weeks later, he found a job at a local printing press; a furtive backdoor arm of a legitimate business. Kevin had worked in printing as a young man, before he became a café manager, so he found the work undemanding and mundane. He was required to work alone and the role lacked the creative expression that he craved. But the job had one plus. Ink. Thick, luxurious and expensive.

Each day, Kevin would clean the equipment and collect the leftover ink. Then, in the long hours of solitude, while the machines clattered their automated heartbeat, Kevin would paint his imaginings on scraps of paper and hang them around the office to dry. It wasn't long until a passing colleague commented "You should be an artist. You're too good to be working here." *I am an artist*, Kevin had silently agreed. And he resigned.

His first step was to create saleable art; glorious watercolour images of the stately terraced houses along Victoria Street. Standing on a street corner in Kings Cross, he sold them all within an hour. Next, he went in search of a day job; one where he could earn a regular income as an artist. It was this search that led him to Mr S.

It was a job in advertising — Kevin assumed he would be sketching artwork for furniture advertisements — and the interview had been harrowing. Five or six men with shrewd eyes and expensive suits had gathered around him and peppered him with questions. As the interview had come to a close, it was Mr S who had approached Kevin with an outstretched hand. "Kevin, you should really just be an artist," he had remarked. And then he had offered him the job.

It wasn't art. It was coordinating advertising and other administrative tasks. Kevin was underwhelmed by the position and walked out within weeks. There was no notice given; no explanation. One day, he just didn't turn up.

I am an artist. Kevin was tired of apologising for his makeshift day jobs. He was sick of being just another guy with a dream. So, when two New Zealand girls at a party asked "What do you do?" he decided to declare it out loud — boldly and proudly: "I'm an artist." And the next day he set about making it happen.

His creations were silk-screen prints, produced on 320gsm Kent paper; black and white prints finished with original watercolour. A local sculptress offered him part of her studio to work from and his art was peddled on the streets of Sydney by his small and imperfectly-formed sales team. It was going well and, Kevin thought, it was about to get a whole lot better.

The offer had come from an old Shepparton acquaintance; a travelling salesman with a smooth voice and shifty eyes. He stumbled into Kings Cross one day and promised Kevin nationwide exposure. "I'll sell these for you," he had crooned. "Put together 30 prints, but I want them framed and ready to hang," the salesman explained.

Kevin obliged. With his meagre savings, he prepared 30 pictures for sale and handed them delicately to his new business partner. It was the last he was to see of his art, or his money. When he later tracked the salesman down, following his path to Albury, he discovered all his paintings had been sold. The salesman had pocketed the funds and used them to migrate to London.

Robbed of all his funds and struggling to establish himself as a bona fide player on the Sydney art scene, Kevin was tiptoeing on the edges of destitution and failure. But all he could hear were the generous words of Mr S: "You should really just be an artist."

It had been many months since the two had spoken; not since Kevin had rudely and abruptly abandoned his advertising job. But Kevin was too desperate to be contrite. Instead, his reaching for help was cocky and courageous. It took one phone call. "I took your advice. I'm an artist now," Kevin declared …

The rain had abated, and the taxi driver was carefully navigating the meandering slopes of Edgecliff. Mr S was too astute to hold grudges; too prudent to demand explanation. He had simply listened as Kevin outlined the nature of his artwork, and the positive sales figures from his Kings Cross stalls. "Bring a few examples to me," Mr S had asked. "Come and see me at my home."

The taxi slowed to a halt and Kevin gently gathered his collection of screen prints from the back seat. They were all he had left in the world; the only thread that connected him with his heart's desire. Slowly, steadily, he emerged from the misty condensation of the taxi and into the grey world.

In front of him as he stood on the shiny bitumen road was an immense sandstone wall — a solid mass of yellow, pink and taupe that towered over its surroundings and threatened to block out every bit of available sky. Fingers of ivy flowed over the top of the wall and spilled down toward the ground in rivulets of dark green. Over the wall, Kevin could glimpse the russet tiles of a large, impressive rooftop; a jumble of angles, eaves and intersections. At the roadside, the expanse of sandstone was broken only by a nondescript wrought iron gate, set low against the footpath. On the left-hand side of the gate, the metal box of a modern intercom system — cold and almost eerie — stared back at him.

In an instant, all Kevin's worlds collided in a single, synchronistic moment. The dream of his youth flooded back into his memory and shimmered with intense reality in front of him. This place — Mr S's home — was the place from his dream. This was the dream from his distant past.

And this was his future. *I am an artist.* Kevin felt the reality of the statement resonate through his body. Then he strode boldly to the gate and pressed the intercom.

After their meeting that day, Mr S became one of Kevin Oxley's greatest champions and financial backers. Through his connections, the businessman placed Kevin's prints in Woolworth's supermarkets nationwide and provided permanent premises from which Kevin could work. Kevin eventually turned his attention to other forms of art. His very first attempt at portraiture — a self-portrait in oil — was hung in the Art Gallery of NSW, at the prestigious Archibald Awards in 1967.

For nearly 50 years, Kevin has established an outstanding reputation in an extraordinary array of art forms including painting, sculpture and printmaking. In June 2014, he was awarded the Medal of the Order of Australia (OAM) for his services to the visual and performing arts. He currently lives on the Sunshine Coast in Queensland and his work hangs in private and public collections around the world, including in the Sydney Opera House, the Prime Minister's Lodge in Canberra, and NSW Parliament House.

Clairvoyance: the mind's eye

Over time, the term clairvoyance has become synonymous with any form of psychic or mystical experience however this common definition is misleading. Clairvoyance is, literally, 'clear vision'. It is only used accurately when it's used to describe psi information that is received as a visual image or representation.

From the divine visions of the Bible and Quran, to the legendary feats of the Oracle of Delphi in Ancient Greece, our history is rich with stories of clairvoyant experiences such as apparitions and visual premonitions. [13]

One modern example of outstanding clairvoyance comes from the US Defence Force and a Chief Warrant

Officer named Joe McMoneagle. For more than five years, McMoneagle was revered as one of the US military's most accurate 'remote viewers' or psychic spies (read more in Chapter 18). One of his most famous (now declassified) successes was his discovery of the yet-to-be-released Russian Typhoon submarine. Throughout the duration of this top secret Russian operation, McMoneagle was able to visualise and therefore provide up-to-date information on the progress of the submarine's manufacture and could recreate detailed images of its cutting-edge technology. He did all of this from the Fort Meade military base in Maryland, USA.

However, McMoneagle's ability to receive and provide detailed psi imagery is widely regarded as exceptional — both by psi researchers and by the US Military (in 1984, McMoneagle was awarded the Legion of Merit medal for his work in remote viewing). For most people, clairvoyant information arrives as fleeting images or hazy inner visions. Except in rare cases, the information is not transferred through the eyes like normal vision but, rather, appears as a visual impression in the mind.

8

The Sudden Awakening
Lafayette IN, USA

Lafayette slept. It was the earliest hour on a Monday and all was still in the Indiana city. The midnight sky hung like velvet overhead and the stars were radiant in the darkness of a new moon. To the east, bleary-eyed drivers floated along the I65. In the city centre, the street lights glowed like rows of fluorescent watchmen.

All appeared quiet and yet underneath the superficial stillness the city hummed with a frantic activity. Lafayette was a college town, it was late August and the students had returned for the beginning of the school year. Matt was one of those students.

Alone in his room, Matt breathed softly in the deep, untroubled sleep of youth. Nothing ever disturbed him too much. An easy-going 22-year-old with an unhurried and philosophical view on life, Matt had just begun his fourth year at Purdue University. Purdue, the "Cradle of Astronauts", home of the mighty Boiler Makers and, Matt hoped, the place where he would someday earn his degree in Computer Engineering. However, like most things in life,

Matt didn't take his studies too seriously. Completing his four-year degree was still a few years off and he was quietly committed to making sure that his education was regularly balanced with a generous dose of fun.

For the past three-and-a-half years, Matt had been meandering toward graduation. For a semester, or maybe two, he would attend college and complete exams. Then, out of a restless necessity, he would take a break — get a job, do work experience or head off on a surfing holiday abroad for six months or so. Then he'd return in time to take up his obligatory studies.

This semester, the Fall Semester of 1995, Matt had decided to return to the halls of Purdue. He had thoroughly enjoyed his summer break, driving a truck and constructing tents for a local marquee company. He was in great physical shape, in love with life and he had saved some money from his summer job. Matt was happy, healthy and ready to get back into some serious study. Well, sort of.

School had been back only a week and Matt's social calendar had already kicked in to a familiar and fun routine. It was the beginning of the football season and football offered 34,000 Purdue students a reason to gather, eat, drink and socialise.

This weekend had been like so many others. Saturday morning had started with the classic college Breakfast Club; a chance for the students to prime their young bodies with pitchers of alcoholic cocktails — Screwdrivers, Bloody Marys and a variety of unidentified concoctions of questionable origin. Later in the day, the rowdy group had stumbled into the student section of the Ross-Ade Stadium where, obnoxious, dishevelled and dressed in ridiculous costumes, they had cheered on the Purdue football team.

Sunday had been devoted to professional football. Matt was not an avid fan of any particular team, but he was always happy to include himself in the festive atmosphere and good-natured banter that accompanied these Sunday outings. After sleeping off his Saturday hangover, Matt and his friends had located a cheap bar where they had watched the game on television while consuming chicken wings and beer in equal quantities. Finally, exhausted and happy after a frantic weekend, Matt had returned to his apartment to sleep.

This year, Matt's younger brother, Jay was also relocating to Lafayette to begin his freshman year at Purdue.[14] He and Matt had grown up in Valparaiso, a small town 80 miles north of Lafayette. Jay was driven from Valparaiso by their parents — wide-eyed and nervous and with the car groaning under the weight of his luggage. In the evening, after Jay had been settled at his fraternity metres away from Matt's apartment, the family had met for dinner at a local restaurant.

Matt had not seen his family for several months. His Dad was the same as ever; even-tempered, stoic and reserved, but the change in his Mum was immediately evident. For as long as Matt could remember, his Mum had dedicated her life to him and Jay. She had encouraged, supported, nurtured and guided her sons, and many of their friends, with an instinctive flair for healing. Of all the people in the world, Matt knew that she alone could listen to him without judgement and fully understand his bohemian nature.

However, since a high school reunion a year ago, Matt's mother had been undergoing a steady metamorphosis. Almost imperceptibly she had lost weight, changed her hair and seemed to be drinking more. With her boys grown up and no longer needing her attention, she had found other outlets for her nurturing nature. By day, she cared for elderly patients and, in her spare time, she comforted an old friend from school — an alcoholic divorcee who lived with his two daughters several hundred miles away. That night at dinner she had been a little tipsy and had seemed overly concerned for Matt's welfare.

"Take care of yourself," she said in the parking lot after dinner. Matt hugged her tightly. "Everything is under control," he replied casually. With one last wave, he watched his parents pull out of the parking lot and drive away into the night. In the weeks that followed, Matt remained blissfully unconcerned about his mother's mid-life transformation. School was starting; there were schedules to review, friends to catch up with and dreams to build.

Now, asleep in his apartment, Matt's mind flickered through pleasant images of parties, pretty girls and chicken wings. He stirred softly in his bed and his lips curved in a faint smile. On the bedside table, the digital clock shone into the darkness and time inched closer toward the dawn of a new week. Outside the window, Lafayette slept. It was 1:30am.

The sensation, when it came, hit Matt like a bullet, reverberating through his body. Sitting bolt upright in the darkness, he gasped with the sudden awakening. Something was wrong. Reality had tilted slightly; there was a disturbance in his world.

Matt struggled to reorient himself to his bedroom surroundings and the strange sense of dread that gnawed at him. Then, within seconds, the experience became acutely physical. Matt clutched at his stomach, cramping and churning, and nausea began to rise up from his belly. In an instant, Matt's emotional unease was forgotten. A violent sickness took hold of his body and he sprung like lightening toward the bathroom.

Matt's body strained against the pain. For the next 20 minutes, he crouched alone on the cold tiled floor and succumbed to the violent seizures of his stomach. His throat burned, his torso ached and all he could think about was the warm comfort of his mother's presence. Matt wanted his Mum now; he wanted her to hold him and soothe him and make him feel better as, Matt knew, only she could. Finally, the nausea abated and Matt, weak and sweating, made his way back to bed.

Lying in his bedroom in the still aftermath of his sickness, Matt finally had time to mull over what had happened to him. *It must have been the chicken wings.* As the physical nausea and emotional unease drained from his body, Matt felt satisfied with this explanation. He pulled the covers up tight, curled his arms around his tender body and drifted off into a deep sleep.

Matt's father visited him the next morning. As he opened the apartment door and saw his father's stern face, Matt's first thought was *Oh no. What have I done this time?* Matt considered the long drive his father must have made to be here, so early in the morning, and he steeled himself for the oncoming tirade. Instead, his father simply guided him downstairs and out into the fresh autumn air.

"Mum's dead." The statement came suddenly, abruptly.

Matt stared blankly at this father, a faint smile of amusement hinting at the corners of his mouth. His Dad must be joking.

"Mum's dead." Again the blunt delivery; again Matt's inability to place any meaning on the words.

"Mum's dead."

Atom by atom, Matt's world started to unravel. The reality of the moment began to scorch itself into Matt's brain and time slowed to an agonising crawl. He saw his father's face, resigned and impassive and felt the earth revolving steadily beneath his feet. Then a raw and primal anger rose up in him, and flowed from a pool of dark grief into his clenched fists.

Matt's mother had not been at home; she was away visiting the divorced friend who had taken up so much of her attention lately. The story was murky. There was news of a break in and a fatal gunshot. Apparently she had been upstairs, alone, and her friend was the first to discover her.

The how and why didn't help Matt. There were just questions, and rage, and the constant screaming in his mind, *She shouldn't have been there! She shouldn't have been there!* But in the blur of information his father offered, one tiny detail shone like neon.

"It happened this morning," his dad was saying, "at around 1:30am." Matt thought of his abrupt awakening, the sense of doom and the violent sickness that had plagued him in the early hours. It seemed incredulous, but had he somehow *felt* his mother dying?

He had little time to dwell on this mystery, as Jay walked up the street to come and meet them. As he heard the news, Jay collapsed at their feet distraught and grief stricken. It was some hours later before the shock wore off and Matt and Jay were able to talk about the tragedy. "What is weird is that I was sick last night," Jay remarked. "At about 1:30am. Really violently ill, as if I had food poisoning."

On Monday, 28 August 1995 at around 1:30am, Matt Omo's beloved mother died from a fatal gunshot wound. As she lay dying, far from home, her two sons woke simultaneously in Lafayette, Indiana and vomited violently in the night. The details surrounding the death of Matt's mother were never fully clarified, nor accepted by all of Matt's family. There was suspicion of foul play, depression and a midnight intruder, however the official investigation concluded that it was a case of tragic suicide.

Matt completed his degree in Computer Engineering but lasted no more than five years in his chosen field. He eventually realised that the greatest gift his mother had given him was a natural capacity for compassion and healing, and he began a career in holistic health.

He spent many years travelling the world, studying alternative therapies and philosophies, and currently owns a holistic healing centre in Sydney, Australia with his wife, Michele.

Telepathy: Mind talk

The idea of mind-to-mind communication has been passed down in human folklore and philosophy for millennia. For instance, the ancient siddhis of Hindu and Buddhist teachings include *para citta ādi abhijñatā*, the ability to know or read the minds of others. The Christian Bible also appears to refer to this skill.[15] However, the term telepathy was not used until 1882, when it was coined by British scholar, Frederic WH Myers. Since then, the idea of telepathy (though always controversial) has sparked the curiosity of many researchers and garnered public support from famous individuals such as Mark Twain and Sigmund Freud.

The term telepathy literally means 'feeling at a distance' however it is generally regarded as different from other forms of psi because the information is *sent* and *received*. For instance, clairsentience (as detailed in Chapter 9) generally involves sensing or feeling something from a distance, however this may include the sense of inanimate objects. In contrast, the study of telepathy centres around a mental signal transmitted by one individual and perceived by another.

It is worth remembering that, as with many psi abilities, our elementary understanding of the telepathic process makes it difficult to clearly define where telepathy ends and other forms of psi begin.

Scientific research into telepathy began in earnest in the late nineteenth century and provided some significant results in favour of its existence. However, many of these studies used techniques that were flawed. They were highly susceptible to inaccuracy, bias and fraud (either conscious or unconscious) and provided sceptics with plausible reasons to doubt. Stronger evidence was provided from 1966, when the Maimonides Centre in New York commenced dream telepathy experiments. Then, in the 1970s, the Ganzfeld technique was introduced to record telepathic experiences in a controlled, clinical and conducive environment. For many, the Ganzfeld research method is highly contentious — mainly because it has become incredibly stringent in its scientific processes and controls. However, it still produces overwhelming evidence for the existence of telepathy.

Meanwhile, outside of the laboratory, stories have regularly surfaced of incredible telepathic feats. Many of the more popular anecdotes tend to feature twins, such as the Jim Twins who were separated at birth. Meeting after 39 years, the twins were astonished to discover the similarities of their life details — they had both been named Jim, had both married a woman called Linda, divorced and then married a woman called Betty. They both had a son named James, with the middle name Allan (although spelt differently) and a dog named Toy.[16] In addition, they shared identical career paths, health issues and habits and, strangely, both had been inspired to build a white picket fence around a tree in their front yards just prior to their reunion.

Anecdotes like this have found some validation in scientific research, which provides strong evidence that twins and couples have a profound ability to connect telepathically. However, it is important to acknowledge that telepathy is not restricted to close family members; complete strangers have also provided stunning evidence of telepathy in a clinical environment.[17] This poses some very interesting questions. If people's thoughts are flying around in the course of our day-to-day lives why do we not 'hear' them? Or, is it that we *are* impacted by the thoughts of others but remain largely unaware of these influences?

Of course, the acceptance of telepathy opens up a Pandora's Box of ethical and legal complications and can easily lead into the murky realms of stage magic and conspiracy. Does sending a mental message mean that people's thoughts can be controlled by a third party? If it is possible to 'read people's minds' are we crossing the boundaries of acceptable privacy? Although research has shown beyond reasonable doubt that telepathy exists, it seems unlikely that instances of mind control or reading specific thoughts occur with regular success. For now, all that science has been able to ascertain for sure is that telepathy is best received when the mind is alert, relaxed and deprived of sensory stimulation.[18]

The story of Matt's mother appears to be a case of *crisis telepathy* — a phenomena that appears regularly in real life but (for obvious reasons) is difficult to replicate in the laboratory. In these cases, it appears that a telepathic connection is initiated (perhaps unconsciously) as a person endures pain or trauma. As with other psi experiences, it seems that the emotion of the crisis increases the intensity of the psi 'signal' and somehow makes it more accessible.

Couple this with the fact that both Matt and his brother were sleeping at the time (an optimal state to receive psi information) and it is easy to see why both brothers had extreme telepathic reactions to their mother's thoughts and experiences, at the exact time of her death.

9

A Heavy Void
Sydney NSW, Australia

It was Monday and the city was alive with expectation. The sweltering heatwave of early February had finally subsided and the people of Sydney were breathing easier as they milled on beaches and in parks, and strolled along the harbour foreshore.

Sydneysiders love their harbour — from the iconic arches of the Harbour Bridge to the sprawling rooftops of the harbourside mansions; the glistening peaks of the Opera House and the bustling ferries of Circular Quay. Sydney is a hive of life and activity and, at the very centre of the city, the harbour is its beating heart.

For several years Jacqueline and her husband Colin had run a successful roading and logistics consultancy out of Auckland, New Zealand. Just a year earlier they had set their sights on developing their business across the Tasman Sea, in Australia. It quickly became apparent that this would require a full-time presence in Sydney.

The idea of relocating to a new country did not faze either Jacqueline or Colin. They were bold and savvy people and Sydney was only a short flight from home. However, packing up and moving from New Zealand was not as simple as it seemed. Although Jacqueline was free to live in Australia, her two children were not.

Jacqueline had met Colin two years after separating from her first husband. As their relationship had deepened so, too, had Colin's connection with Jacqueline's children, Theo and Liv. Over the years, the family unit had become incredibly close and Colin had become a treasured and respected stepfather.

Jacqueline always encouraged Theo and Liv to keep up regular contact with her ex-husband. She believed it was vital that they maintain a good relationship with their father, even if her own choice had been to build a life away from him. She was compassionate and reasonable and aware that her children had their own needs; needs that were sometimes at odds with her own. When a court ordered that the children were not to live outside New Zealand, away from their father, Jacqueline had readily accepted the restriction as fair and just.

So, when it had become apparent that their business needed a presence in Sydney, the family took the only sensible option available to them. Colin agreed to commute to Australia each week and Jacqueline would remain in New Zealand with the children. Theo, a mature 12-year-old, decided he would like to go to boarding school in Christchurch, a two-hour flight from Auckland. There, he would have an opportunity to receive an excellent education and also be closer to his father, who lived locally.

Jacqueline and nine-year-old Liv stayed behind in Auckland.

For an entire year, Jacqueline, Colin and the children endured the complications of a being a long-distance family: Auckland — Christchurch — Sydney. On the weekends and during school holidays, they would fly the short distances to be together. In those 12 months the family managed only a few, precious days when they were all together as a unit. It was far from perfect but Jacqueline and Colin could see no other way. Eventually, it was young Liv that provided a suitable alternative.

For several months, Liv had quietly observed Theo's experience at boarding school. He had shared stories of weekend outings and activities, and the good friendships he was making. To Liv, now a strong and independent 10-year-old, this seemed perfect; a continual slumber party with lots of fun and adventure. By the end of the school year, Liv was sure that she wanted to go to boarding school too and Jacqueline set about making it happen.

Jacqueline had missed Colin dreadfully over the past year — the couple were madly in love, and adored spending time together — so it was decided that, with both children now in boarding school, she would live in Sydney during the school terms. On week days, she and Colin would share a cosy inner-Sydney apartment. On regular weekends, she would fly to Christchurch to be with her children. In the school holidays, the family hoped to gather together at their house in Auckland.

For Jacqueline, Christchurch was the perfect place for her children to attend boarding school. Not only were they close to their father, but it was also Jacqueline's home town. In Christchurch Theo and Liv would have the support of her extended family and some of her closest friends. It was also a safe environment. Christchurch was New Zealand's second largest city, with a population nearing 400,000, yet it boasted a crime rate lower than many other cities around the country.

The family threw themselves wholeheartedly into their new lifestyle. At the beginning of the school year Jacqueline took the children to Christchurch to settle them into their schools — Theo at Christ College, one of the oldest and most prestigious high schools in New Zealand, Liv at Selwyn House, a slightly younger school, in the inner suburbs.

After a week in Christchurch, and with her children happy and excited about the coming year, Jacqueline boarded a plane to Sydney, eager to begin the new chapter in her life.

Throughout the summer months cruise ships often dock near Sydney's famous Circular Quay, spewing hordes of wide-eyed tourists into the surrounding cafes and souvenir shops. This summer alone had seen the arrival of 150 ships and over 300,000 passengers. But the city was about to experience something unprecedented. For the first time in history, two grand dames of the Cunard Line would be docking side-by-side in a foreign port. In the morning,

Sydney would be welcoming both the Queen Elizabeth and the majestic Queen Mary 2.

The city was buzzing with the news, and Jacqueline was brimming with anticipation. Sydney harbour was the focus of even more attention than usual.

Jacqueline adored cruising. She and Colin had made several voyages in the past and, in her mind, there were few pleasures as grand as exploring foreign waters on a majestic cruise ship. It was her greatest intention that someday she would sail on the ultimate cruise liner; one day, Jacqueline was certain, she would sail the world on the Queen Mary 2. Tomorrow, her dream ship was docking within a few blocks of her apartment, and there was no way she was going to miss its arrival.

She visualised the entire experience in her mind. She saw herself and Colin strolling down Phillip St toward Circular Quay. They would eat breakfast at a quaint waterside restaurant, and watch the sun rise over the harbour entrance. From there, they would make their way along the Quay and join the crowds waiting to cheer and wave as the two ships docked.

Jacqueline could already feel the sense of celebration. She felt like a child on Christmas Eve, bursting with excitement. In the morning, she would watch her dream ship sail into port and her introduction to Sydney would feel complete. In a final gesture of anticipation, she carefully chose the clothes she would wear and piled them neatly beside the bed. On top, she placed her walking shoes.

She awoke before sunrise to a soft kiss and an eager "Good morning" from Colin. For a fleeting moment, as her body crossed the threshold into wakefulness, Jacqueline was consumed with pure excitement. The moment was here; today was the day!

However, as she rose into a sitting position, her mood suddenly changed. She felt something clunk deep inside her belly. Within a heartbeat, all of her excitement and vigour disappeared and she was left feeling heavy, empty and deflated. Her enthusiasm for the day ahead was gone and her body felt lifeless and drained.

Slumping back onto her pillows, Jacqueline succumbed to the overpowering sensations. It was as if all her energy had retracted into the core of her body. Where there had been exhilaration, just seconds before, now there was a heavy void. She felt empty.

"I don't think I can be bothered going," Jacqueline murmured. She pulled the blankets up round her chin and sank low into her pillows.

Colin was stunned. "But it was your idea to go. Are you alright?"

Jacqueline was aware of how irrational her behaviour seemed but an overwhelming weariness had claimed her body and her emotions. She was unable to muster any energy or enthusiasm. In that moment she could think of nothing worse than getting out of bed. She sensed all her energy caving in on itself. She felt like she had been sucked dry, like a raisin in the sun.

"I don't know what's happened," she admitted. "I just don't want to go out at all. I want to stay here all day."

Jacqueline searched for a logical reason to explain the strange lethargy that had overcome her. She had just left her children in another country. She was still acclimatising to a foreign city. She was flying to Christchurch the next day and had a lot to do before then. *Homesickness, empty nest syndrome, stress?*

With a concerned frown Colin gave Jacqueline a gentle kiss and left the apartment. He would have to watch the arrival of the Cunard liners without her.

As concerned as she was about disappointing Colin, Jacqueline was grateful to be alone. Whatever had taken hold of her, it demanded all of her attention, and right now the outside world was an unwelcome distraction. She checked the clock. 6:45am. It was still early and she was certain sleep would help.

Whenever Jacqueline was indecisive or confused, it had become her practice to take a short nap. In the quietness of sleep, her brain seemed to work through any confusing or complicated circumstances and she always woke with a sense of clarity. Jacqueline was sure that after a nap, the reason for her current discomfort would become apparent. As the first rays of daylight flickered against her bedroom window, Jacqueline closed her eyes and drifted back off to sleep.

She woke two hours later, transitioning from deep sleep into a terrifying reality. From the moment she opened her eyes, Jacqueline was aware of a suffocating sense of impending doom. Something was wrong; terribly wrong. As always, her sleep had clarified her situation but this time it was apparent that there was something dark and dangerous lurking in her life. Jacqueline had no idea what the danger was but she knew instinctively that it involved her children.

Jacqueline checked the clock. 8:50am. She was terrified; petrified. Every fibre of her being told her that Theo and Liv were in grave danger and she desperately wanted to be in Christchurch, protecting them. Jacqueline's eyes welled with tears and her mind whirled with panic. *They're in the wrong place. We shouldn't be separated. I shouldn't have left them. This needs to be put right.* In a sudden rush of comprehension, Jacqueline felt an urgent call to action. *I have to be with my children,* she thought, *right now*!

As a deep dread overwhelmed her senses, Jacqueline fought to regain control by applying logic and science. In the past she had worked as a registered nurse and she called upon her medical training to carefully and deliberately assess her situation. Her body seemed to be in shock; her heart was racing and she was restless and uneasy. At the same time, she felt like she was anchored in place. Every part of her body felt heavy, as if stuck in concrete. As much as she wanted to, Jacqueline could not find the strength to get out of bed.

Everything is fine, she reassured herself. *I am being ridiculous. I'm flying to Christchurch tomorrow for a week. They have their father, grandparents and extended family around them. They're safe. Besides,* she rationalised further, *they're in completely different locations, several kilometres apart. Nothing's going to happen to both of them.*

But she could not dismiss the sensation that her children were in trouble. She felt desperate, and in the end she surrendered to exasperation and irrationality. *Fine,* she thought, *I'll catch the earliest flight I can and go to Christchurch today!*

Jacqueline's body responded immediately; it was as if someone had flicked a switch. Energy flowed back into her veins and her motivation suddenly returned. She bounced out of bed and began preparations for the day ahead.

It was 10.45, and Jacqueline was just completing her morning exercise regime, when her mobile phone beeped with a text message. Then another. And another. And again. And again. She picked up her phone. Within a heartbeat, fear and dread returned to consume her. There, on the screen were several notifications from her closest friends in New Zealand, each of them relaying the same, horrifying message:

Massive earthquake in Christchurch! Buildings are down everywhere. Lots of dead. Where are you, Jacqueline? Where are the children?

Trembling and weak, Jacqueline found the remote and turned on the television. The scene that greeted her was terrifying. The quake had happened only minutes before and the news cameras were struggling to capture the extent of the damage. Christchurch Cathedral, located metres from

Theo's school and built in the same era, lay in ruins. The city was in chaos, and bloodied and frightened residents were everywhere. Throughout the city, buildings had collapsed on unsuspecting inhabitants and the ground was pitted with deep cracks and liquefaction.

Her instinct had been chillingly on target — her children were in grave danger and her only thought was to be with them.

Jacqueline stumbled around the apartment erratically packing luggage and praying that she could get to Christchurch quickly. It was now an hour since the quake and still no word from Theo or Liv. Heading for the airport Jacqueline was in shock and panic. There were only two things that she knew for certain — she was going to make it to Christchurch, no matter what, and, once there, she could be going to a funeral.

On Tuesday, 22 February 2011, shortly before sunrise, the Queen Mary 2 and Queen Elizabeth arrived in Sydney Harbour. A few hours later, across the Tasman Sea, the city of Christchurch was struck by a violent and deadly earthquake. The exact time of the quake was recorded as 12:51pm (NZDS), approximately five hours after Jacqueline first woke with an acute sense of fatigue and unease. Measuring 6.6M$_L$ on the Richter scale and centred at a shallow depth, the quake demolished several inner-city buildings and left many others uninhabitable. 185 lives were lost, crushed in the rubble of Christchurch's historic buildings.

Jacqueline received word from Theo and Liv as she waited to board her flight to Auckland. They were both relatively unharmed and had sought shelter with friends. After a day's travel, Jacqueline was finally reunited with her children at Christchurch airport. They departed the city immediately and eventually flew back to Sydney. With their father's consent, the children were ultimately permitted to settle permanently in Australia.

Clairsentience: Sensational psi

Clairsentience is the term used to describe the experience of receiving intuitive knowledge or information as an emotion, feeling or physical sensation. It literally means 'clear feeling'.

Of all the ways in which humans perceive psi information, the manifestation of feelings and emotions appears to be the most profound. Even our language is littered with phrases that suggest that we have an ability to feel the essence of a situation. *I had a gut instinct; I can feel it in my bones; that person makes my blood boil.*

Research indicates that these phrases are more than just poetic descriptions. Many studies have demonstrated that our bodies literally respond physically and physiologically to psi information, *even if we are unconsciously aware of these reactions.*

For instance, neuroscientist, Leanna Standish, recorded unconscious telepathy in the brains of 30 separate pairs of participants.[19] One participant was subjected to an occasional flickering light, while their partner was closely monitored in a distant fMRI scanner. The unconscious reactions in the monitored participants were incredible. Not only did their brains react to their partner's flickering light, but they reacted *in their visual cortex* in particular; their brains reacted as if they were viewing the light themselves.

It is interesting to note that the gut appears to have a close association with psi-based emotions. Jacqueline's case is a clear example of this. She had a distinct 'clunking' sensation in her belly, long before she began thinking consciously of her children. In 2005, Dr Dean Radin explored this concept in a clinical telepathy experiment.[20] Testing a group of adult couples, Radin discovered that a participant's gut would become more active (i.e., start churning) when their isolated partner was subjected to high emotion.

Clairsentience can manifest in the following ways:
- physical sensations, particularly in the gut
- physiological reactions such as sweating, elevated heart rate and fatigue
- profound or distinct emotions
- a strong pulling or yearning to undertake a course of action, or move in a certain direction.

10

A Sense of Dread
Strathfield NSW, Australia

One Southern Fried Chicken Burger meal deal, upsized, with a Pepsi Max

It was a cool April night and Mat Beeche was on his way home from evening class at university. The staff at CC's Chargrill knew Mat well and, before he had even stepped through the door, preparation had begun on his usual meal. Dinner at CC's had become a regular habit — it was only a few steps across the Strathfield Plaza as he stepped off the train, the welcome was warm and familiar and there was always free food on offer. All thanks to Mat's weeping mother.

Mat had discovered CC's on his first day in this western Sydney suburb — over a year earlier. Leaving rural New South Wales to study in the big city had been a huge transition for 18-year-old Mat, and his Mum and Dad had come along for support. They'd been to see Mat's new school, a renowned performing arts college, and settled him into his new home. By late afternoon of that long and arduous day, Mat's mother sat at an outdoor table at CC's

Chargrill, with her cappuccino. But, no longer able to disguise her worry, she dissolved in a torrent of tears.

At that moment, with the efficiency of a ward nurse, Carol Christodoulides, swooped in on their table to find out why one of her customers was in tears. "Are you alright?" she enquired in a thick, Greek accent. Through muffled sobs Mat's mother explained that they were from the country and now, her eldest was leaving home, knowing nobody in the big city.

"Don't you worry," Mrs Christodoulides soothed, "I'll take care of him." And she had. At least three times a week, for the past 16 months, Mat had stopped at CC's for his evening meal and, inevitably, Mrs Christodoulides would pile extra food into his carry bags. "Here's a lasagne for later in the week. Have some vegetables, and a salad for your lunches." Life as a struggling student had many drawbacks for Mat but, thanks to Mrs Christodoulides, going hungry was not ever one of them.

Tonight, however, Mrs Christodoulides was not in her restaurant. It was Con, her husband, who greeted Mat and he hadn't been party to the promises to a weeping mother. He was not interested in handouts to out-of-town students. Tonight, Mat would get what he paid for, and no more.

"One Southern Fried Chicken Burger meal deal, upsized, with a Pepsi Max." Within minutes, Mat's dinner was prepared and packed in a plastic carry bag. Slipping the handle casually over one arm, Mat set off home with the aroma of freshly fried chicken wafting up from his bag.

Mat strode out of the Plaza and made his way north along Elva Street. The walk home was relatively short and easy, especially for someone as young and fit as Mat. Although he'd graduated from his performing arts high school, and was now studying psychology at university, his tall frame still showed the signs of years of intense activity; exercise classes, Pilates and dance lessons. He was also strong — the result of eight years of martial arts training. Though he'd not practised Tai Kwon Do since arriving in Sydney, there was a black belt hanging in his closet.

Mat shared an apartment on the grounds of St Anne's Anglican Church. In return for cheap accommodation, Mat had agreed to teach Sunday School to a bunch of wide-eyed pre-schoolers who were bemused and thrilled to be taught Bible passages from this young Catholic man, who also frequented the bars and nightclubs of Sydney's Oxford Street. Somehow, the arrangement worked and those comfortable rooms at the back of St Anne's Church were home.

Eager to get there, Mat covered ground swiftly and with purpose — his red Havaianas "flupped" through the night air. Flup, flup, flup. Mat strode toward the intersection and his usual shortcut down tree-lined Albert Road. Flup, flup, flup. He continued unabated, but an anxious energy was growing and as the street sign came into view, Mat felt distinctly uncomfortable about taking Albert Road. It was hard to pinpoint, but he had a sense of dread. A sense he should take the long way; up the well-lit path of Elva Street.

As he continued walking, the emotion inside of Mat turned distinctly physical. A feeling rose in the pit in his stomach; a rumbling, like nervous butterflies. Mat stopped sharply at the intersection and stared into the dim shadows of Albert Road.

For a few moments, Mat assessed his strange feeling. It was a bit like guilt or remorse. *Have I done something I shouldn't have? Have I been rude to somebody? Have I said something I shouldn't have?* Mat replayed the day in his head, searching for a reason for his anxiety, his nervous tension, but he could not make sense of his feelings or see anything that made him anxious or fearful. He shrugged and dismissed the strange sensation and started down the Albert Road shortcut.

As he walked all was still and quiet. In the evening darkness, light glowed from the windows of houses and apartments. Giant bats shuffled in the large brush box trees lining the street. He was minutes from home. In the distance, Mat noticed two men sitting on a low brick fence and, in that moment, everything crystallised.

Time slowed to a crawl and Mat, giving into the feeling he'd resisted, became consumed with dread, anxiety and a strange sense of déjà vu. *You are going to be mugged.* The thought was clear and direct and, inevitable.

In those brief seconds, Mat's logical mind was still struggling to take control. He knew he could walk away, right now, and be safe. But somehow, his brain refused to acknowledge the knowing that had consumed him. *If they come toward you, you can cross the road,* his inner voice was saying. *Don't be afraid of them. You don't know them. What you are feeling doesn't make sense.*

But another part of Mat knew the truth. *These men are going to mug you,* it was saying. *They're going to ask you a question; they're going to talk to you. You're going to have an altercation with these men.*

It took only a few steps for Mat to reach the two men. In one swift movement they were up and beside him. Mat felt a hand grip his shoulder, "Hey bro. Give us your money." Mat flicked the hand away and tried to walk on, "I don't have any money." Both men blocked his path, one in front and one behind. One was about Mat's height, but slimmer. The other was solid and bulky and at least a head taller than Mat. This was the one to be wary of, he knew. Pushing them aside he said, "I told you, I don't have any money."

The headlock came suddenly and from behind. In an instant, the big man's arms were wrapped around Mat's neck and he was struggling against the violent hold. "Give us your money or you're going to get cut," said the smaller man.

In that moment, the dread and unease drained from Mat's body. This was it; the situation his awareness had been warning him about, and what he needed now was a clear head.

Time slowed and each moment was separate and defined. Mat's thoughts were calm and rational, almost as if he was standing beside his own body, assessing and offering logical solutions. He became aware of the satchel of university books over his right shoulder. He pulled it in front of his chest, thinking that it would protect him if he were stabbed. The plastic carry bag with his chicken dinner hung over the wrist of his left arm — now both his hands were free.

Mat spoke slowly and deliberately, "Listen, I told you I don't have any money. I just spent my last $8.50 on this chicken burger." The grip tightened, "Give us your phone; and your money."

The years of Tai Kwon Do training streamed into Mat's consciousness. *You know how to get out of this. Just use the big guy's weight against him to free yourself. Just get him off balance.* Mat acted without delay. Full of adrenalin and sure of his ability, he flipped the larger man off his back, manoeuvred behind him and pushed both men over the low brick wall. Then, running for his life, Mat sprinted to the safety of St Anne's Church.

The church hall was busy that night and, by the time the pursuing assailants had caught up with him, Mat was safely nestled in a bustle of children's activities and gossiping parents. The police were called and, while enjoying his still-hot chicken from CC's Chargrill, Mat gave them a detailed description of both attackers.

The two had been described in relation to several crimes in the local area, but were able to avoid capture. They were never brought to justice for their assault on Mat.

Two years later the same sense of dread and guilt returned as Mat walked across an overbridge at the Homebush train station. Consumed by the familiar anxiety and foreboding, Mat looked up to see one of his attackers — the large man who had held him in the headlock — standing in a family group, less than 100 metres away. The police may never have known the identity of these men, but it seems that Mat's intuitive awareness most certainly did.

Psi Missing: Believe it and you will see it

Studies show that if you believe in psi, then you are more likely to be able to use these abilities effectively. In fact, one of the most consistent patterns to emerge from modern psi research is the intriguing affect that deep-set beliefs can have on the results of psi experiments.

The influence of personal belief systems on psi experiment results was first noted by parapsychologist, Gertrude Schmeidler in 1943. Before her experiments, she had cleverly identified participants who believed in psi (sheep) and those who did not (goats). All participants were then given a simple psi task to complete — testing telepathy, precognition or some other form of psi ability. Perhaps unsurprisingly, those who believed that they were capable of fulfilling the tasks (the sheep) consistently scored higher than expected. That is to say, they got more answers correct than would be expected by chance. However, the goats — the sceptics and the non-believers — produced the most intriguing results. Some scored at the rate of chance, implying that all answers were simply guesses, but many other goats scored much lower than they should have. Put simply, those who did not believe in psi were choosing *incorrect answers* many more times than would be expected by chance. One explanation for this is that they received some form of psi information about which answer to choose but, in order to uphold the belief that psi is not possible, their conscious mind deliberately avoided choosing that correct answer.

The concept of a sheep-goat effect — the idea that personal beliefs can either help or hinder the accuracy of psi processes — has been evidenced time and time again since Gertrude Schmeidler's first observation. Researchers now describe the negative results of an experiment as 'psi missing'. These results are as statistically significant as overwhelming 'hits' because they do not reflect the standard expectations of chance. They also hint at an unconscious belief that leads the participant (or participants) to sabotage the results of the experiment.

It is reasonable to assume that 'psi missing' is evident in psi ability in all circumstances — not simply in the laboratory. In 2005, young Mat Beeche was overwhelmed with a sense of dread; an overt warning that he was not to take his usual shortcut home. Even when presented with the opportunity to avoid the coming conflict, Mat's conscious mind refused to be swayed by his intuitive awareness. He consciously chose to ignore the clear, physical, warning signs and, as a result, walked straight into danger.

The sheep-goat affect and psi-missing are surprising and remarkable discoveries of psi research. They hint, not only at the amazing ability all humans have to receive psi information, but also of the incredible power the mind has to ignore psi, if it doesn't fit the way we choose to view the world.

11

Connie's Hunch
Chicago IL, USA

Connie wanted the Stevens.

It had first caught his eye back in the spring of 1939, just after he opened in New Mexico, and he had been researching the hotel ever since. He had gathered information in his usual way; secretly, covertly, snooping around like some underworld private investigator. He called it stalking. He was good at it, and it was effective.

For the past three years, he had laboured through government papers, immersed himself in the financial records and met with trustees and shareholders in secret. Now, as he stood staring through the rain onto the bleak Chicago skyline, Connie knew everything there was to know about the Stevens Chicago Hotel.

Designed in the classic *Beaux-Arts* style, it was the largest hotel in the world. It boasted 3000 guest rooms and 3000 baths. The banqueting hall could cater for up to 8000 guests. The hotel had its own hospital — two wards and an operating theatre — and a dry cleaning department that could service 500 suits a day. Its guests were treated to an in-house cinema, a bowling alley and a rooftop miniature golf course. It could accommodate the population of a small town and, as the lively young manager had eagerly offered, "It would take eight hours a day for a full month to see every room in the building." The Stevens Hotel was massive, it was ostentatious, and Connie wanted it.

The only problem was that he couldn't have it.

The Great Depression had been unrelenting on the American hotel industry and the Stevens had not been immune. By the time Connie had set his sights on it, the Stevens family had gone bankrupt, the government had taken the company into receivership and the grandest hotel on the planet — originally built for $30 million — had plummeted to a value of just $7 million. But even at that price, it was out of Connie's reach. As astute as he was, his ability to raise capital was limited to smaller investors and his cash on hand was only $300,000.

Then, last December, the playing field changed again. Pearl Harbour was bombed, the United States entered World War II and, almost immediately, the Air Force swooped in and purchased the Stevens Hotel to house its growing squadrons.

Connie watched the raindrops bump and merge on the misty window pane, and lightly drummed his fingers against his thigh. The hotel he coveted more than any other was now nothing more than a luxury military base. Its bedrooms were now barracks; its massive function space was a maze of training rooms, and Connie's dream of owning the greatest hotel on Earth was slowly slipping away. But it wasn't dead yet.

While the Stevens Hotel was the company flagship the Stevens Corporation held other assets, tax claims and accounts receivable; a jumble of administrative responsibilities that the military department had acquired with their purchase but could certainly do without in war time. So, the Air Force took the building but put everything else up for sale.

Connie jumped at the chance. "If I can't have the hotel, I'll have the corporation." It was a shrewd move and one he hoped would put him in prime position to purchase the hotel if, and when, the government ever released it. In the meantime, maybe he could make a buck or two from the assets.

Ultimately, the trustees had asked for sealed bids on the company. Connie detested sealed bids — in his opinion any decent businessman should — and as soon as he had made his initial bid of $165,000 Connie knew that figure was a mistake. Something about it didn't feel right to him. His gut feelings were being tested, but they'd never let him down before.

'Connie's Hunches' had become an institution amongst his locker room friends and boardroom buddies. Because of their frequency, and their accuracy, Connie had spent hours trying to work out exactly what the feelings were and where they came from. He was aware of how closely they resembled the premonitions of a crystal ball gazer but, in his mind, they were not a mystical experience;

they were natural insights. He was sure that everyone had them, whether they were aware of them or not.

In the end, Connie had settled on a definition that suited his strong Christian faith and appeased the curious. His hunches, he advised everyone, were like an answered prayer. He would do the best he could with his logical mind — he would think, research and plan — and then he'd simply ask God, *What would you have me do?*

Sometimes the answer would be instantaneous, sometimes it would take hours, but Connie had come to trust his hunches and was happy to sit in what he called his "inner silence" until the answer, like a mini-epiphany, popped into his head.

That's what he had done with the Stevens Corporation bid. Intuitively knowing that the original figure was wrong, Connie had spent most of the night pondering and listening intently to what his inner voice was telling him. It was saying he needed more: $180,000. The figure kept running through his head. It felt right, it felt fair, and Connie was satisfied. The next day, even as the early morning fog lifted off Lake Michigan, he changed his bid.

Now, on this dismal Chicago day, he anxiously waited for news.

He sighed deeply. The rain had finally abated and a small finger of sunlight was playing with the raindrops on the windowpane, turning them into glittering orbs of gold. He was lost in their gilded beauty and didn't hear the footsteps until his assistant was at his shoulder. The first thing Connie saw was the envelope, stamped with the seal of the Stevens trustees.

"Did I get it?" he asked.

The assistant smiled broadly. "Yes, you did Sir, but it was very close. The next bidder went in at $179,800 — you won by only $200."

Connie closed his eyes and thanked his God and the silent voice that had led him one step closer to his dream. "That hotel's going to be mine someday, boy!" he shouted jubilantly. "Break out the champagne!"

The assistant beamed as he turned to oblige.

"Absolutely," he said. "Congratulations, Mr Hilton!"

Conrad Hilton took possession of the Stevens Corporation in 1942 and ultimately made a $2 million profit on the assets. The US government eventually put the Stevens Hotel on the market (by this stage, an empty shell of a building) in 1944. Hilton didn't bite, thinking that he would get a better deal when the war was over, and openly regretted not listening to his intuition in that instance. It was a year, and many millions of dollars, later that he finally managed to purchase the largest hotel in the world.

In 1951, six years after he bought it, the Stevens Hotel was renamed the Hilton Chicago. It still stands today on Michigan Avenue; a proud part of US history and a remarkable monument to Conrad Hilton — an astute businessman who is remembered for both his hotels and his hunches.

Interpreting psi: Right brain domain

Our current scientific understanding of psi is still in its infancy, but there is growing consensus that wherever this non-local information comes from, it manifests via our unconscious mind. Therefore, to become aware of this information, we need to perceive and interpret it with our conscious mind.

Researchers are increasingly noting that interpreting psi appears to be a right-brain process — akin to creativity, intuition and emotion. For this reason, left-brain processes such as critical thinking, logic and reason appear to inhibit the flow of psi information as it is interpreted.[21]

Just as musicians are most effective when they are in a creative 'flow', research shows that psi information appears to be more accurate and extraordinary when the logical mind is either neutralised or ignored; when the information is allowed to be received without the need to analyse, label or control it. In Conrad Hilton's case, he speaks of deliberately quieting his mind and patiently waiting for an answer. By doing so, he allowed his psi messages to be interpreted unfiltered, unhurried and unhindered.

12

A Determined Future
Oahu HI, USA

Although John was only 17 years old, he had already lived a whole lot of life. John was already well acquainted with both success and failure — limitations, ridicule, loss, excellence, despair, freedom, weakness, pain, frustration, but always the unconditional love of his parents. He had known desire and determination and the sweet success of fulfilling a dream. But he had never known inspiration. Not like this.

The year was 1972. And a man called Paul C. Bragg, whom John had never heard of before, was permanently, profoundly, changing his life. Earlier this week, Bragg's photo had beckoned to him from the small flyer on the door of the local health food store. It was the word 'yoga' in the ad – INTRODUCTORY YOGA CLASS: Special Guest Speaker – that first caught his eye. But more than that, it was something in the face of Paul Bragg that compelled John to attend.

So here he was at the Sunset Recreation Hall on the North Shore of Oahu. It was not a large gathering. As the class progressed, John's muscles cramped and his towel mat did nothing to cushion him against the hard floor. But none of those things mattered. John was mesmerized by the words and the quiet conviction of Paul Bragg. For the first time in his life, John was swept by a wave of deep, palpable inspiration.

I want to be like him. I want to teach. I want to inspire. I want to be intelligent. John's reaction to Bragg's speech was immediate, emphatic and completely at odds with what John knew about life.

John Demartini was born and raised in Houston, Texas. From the moment he entered the world, it was clear that his path was not going to be an easy one. John's physical abnormalities were clearly visible at birth; one arm and a leg turned inward at an unnatural angle. His speech impediment became evident by the age of three as he struggled to pronounce words clearly and effectively. By the time he started school, at six, John's dyslexia and learning difficulties were undeniable.

John was forced to wear a brace until he was four but eventually overcame his physical deformity. His subsequent yearning for freedom was acute and deeply rooted. However, it was his learning difficulties — his dyslexia, his illiteracy, his inability to make sense of words — that proved to have a greater impact on his future and his self-esteem.

John's first grade teacher had sown the first seed. "John will never amount to anything," she announced. And so it was that John was condemned to the ranks of the stupid, the useless and the completely unteachable. He adopted clever strategies to cope with his challenges. He asked the smart students to explain things to him verbally. And he learned how to play sport well — too well. At times, his prowess was too much for opposing teams to bear and he would be beaten off-field for daring to excel.

Then he discovered surfing — a sport he could enjoy on his own terms. But by the time he was 14, John had quit school and was living on the streets. Eventually, his craving for freedom coupled with his passion for surfing (and his lack of prospects) won out. He knew what he wanted to do; he wanted to surf. John asked his parents to drop him off on the interstate so he could hitchhike to California. They lovingly but tearfully obliged.

In California, John did whatever he needed to survive, and he surfed. He lived on the streets and the beaches and panhandled for money. However, it wasn't long before the big waves of Hawaii lured him offshore and, saving just enough funds for a one-way flight, he landed in Honolulu. The waves were certainly bigger here and day-to-day life was a familiar routine. By day he would surf, at night he would sleep in whatever shelter he had secured for himself; under a bridge near Sunset Beach, on a park bench in Ehukai Beach Park, in restrooms, abandoned cars and homes, or in makeshift tent structures.

During these years, his surfing made him lean and athletic, but John's undoing was his diet. Grazing on whatever food he could gather, including edible roadside plants, John eventually succumbed to poisoning. Cyanide.

Strychnine. The pain and convulsions that wracked his body were excruciating and deadly. If he had not been found by chance one day, asphyxiating alone in his tent, John would have died. But someone *did* find him and nursed him back to health. She introduced him to the local health food store and that eventually led him to this gathering with Paul Bragg, renowned nutritionist and holistic health pioneer.

When Bragg finished his talk he invited the attendees to sit in 10 minutes of quiet self-reflection. Ten minutes to decide what they wanted to dedicate their lives to. Ten minutes to decide their destiny. It was a huge ask for a 17-year-old but, with every cell in John's body reverberating with inspiration and belief, he was ready and eager. In fact, it took only seconds for John to reject everything he had been taught to believe about himself. *I want to understand Universal Laws and the link between mind, body and spirit. I want to be free, and travel, and explore the world. I want to do what this guy does,* he silently declared. *I want to teach, because that's what intelligent people do. I want to inspire in the way I am being inspired.*

John's newfound conviction stayed with him as Bragg began to speak softly from the front of the room. "It is time for a guided imagery meditation," he advised. Bragg's voice was steady and soothing and it was not long before John was basking in a state of deep relaxation. Within minutes, the pain in his limbs subsided and his mind became still and calm. The soft sounds of the room began to drift out of his awareness and …

The room was gone. In an instant, John was transported and found himself far from his homeless existence and crippled body in Hawaii. Instead, he stood in front of an imposing stone archway in an unknown city. On either side of the arch, two men stood like sentinels; upright and attentive. Striding confidently and with purpose, John walked through the archway and out into the space beyond. He found himself on a balcony, alone, several storeys above the ground. The afternoon sun glinted through city buildings, casting angular shadows across a wide piazza. In the distance, the cityscape expanded in an array of windows, columns and spires, and rows of leafy trees swayed gently in the breeze. Below him, standing shoulder to shoulder on the open ground, a million people watched and waited. They were there to see him — to hear him speak and to learn from him.

To John, nothing was surprising about the scene, yet it was not expected either. It simply was what it was; natural, comfortable and familiar. As soon as he arrived, an expectant hush settled over the crowd and without hesitation, John began to speak. His words flowed easily, as if from a deep well of knowledge and experience. His voice was rich and strong. His message was wise and sincere and he spoke of the human ability to heal; of hope and empowerment and of living with a mission. He was inspired, and he was inspiring.

This was not a diseased young man dreaming of a brighter future. This was John Demartini educated, wise and esteemed.

It was many moments before John's vision began to fade and his mind slowly reorientated itself back to the yoga class. But even as reality returned, the awesome truth of what he had just witnessed reverberated through his body and tears began to well. Opening his eyelids, John gazed around the room slowly and revelled in the awesome wonder that he saw reflected on every face there. At the front of the room, Paul Bragg sat in complete stillness, looking skyward with an expression that signified complete grace and contentment.

John was changed — no longer content to be the boy who couldn't read or write, the cripple or the beach bum without a future. With the vision still misty in his eyes and the grace of Paul Bragg emanating throughout the room, John settled into a new sense of personal conviction. He had not read a book, nor completed school, but he knew that he was going to prove his first grade teacher wrong. John Demartini was going to amount to something great.

For the next three weeks, John attended morning gatherings with Paul Bragg. On the day Bragg announced his departure from Hawaii, John's immediate response was one of confusion and despair — *how would he ever grow without his mentor to guide him?* However, Bragg's parting gift was to offer John a mantra; a simple declaration for him to repeat daily. *I am a genius and I apply my wisdom.* "Say it every day and never miss a day in your life, son," Bragg had advised. "Soon your body's cells will tingle with it, and so will the world."

In the following years, armed with the knowledge that he was capable of greatness and Bragg's simple affirmation, John set off on a long, determined path toward higher education. He returned to Texas, learned how to read and write, sat and passed the High School Equivalency, entered college and worked towards his first degree. Along the way, he discovered a love of philosophy, psychology and sociology and devoured thousands of books written by history's greatest minds.

Forty-four years from his revelation in the yoga class in Hawaii, Dr John Demartini is now regarded as the world's leading authority on human behaviour and personal development. He has studied hundreds of academic disciplines, read over 29,000 educational writings and authored over 40 books of his own. Ever yearning to be free, Demartini travels the globe continually, living out his vision as a 17-year-old; educating, counselling, teaching and inspiring millions of people around the world.

Psi and the future: Is fortune telling a fallacy?

At some time, most people are exposed to the traditional imagery surrounding psi experience. More often than not, this involves a mystical card reader or crystal gazer offering to reveal 'your fortune'. Many people view those premonitions, such as those from a seer or mystic, as a true picture of their future. One that is both determined and unavoidable.

The concept of a determined future — *determinism* — is an idea that arose in ancient Greece and later influenced everything from human philosophy to religion and science. In early times, it was generally regarded that humans were at the mercy of the predetermined destiny orchestrated by a god or gods. This idea that we have no control over our lives — our futures — is a concept that pervades the human experience.

The notion of determinism was later adopted by scientists (minus the notion of divine will). With the rise of Newtonian physics, arrived the belief that the universe was nothing more than a giant machine following a set and determined path from its inception to its ultimate demise. Humans, as nothing more than physical constructions, were at the mercy of the laws of physics and had no ability to prevent, adjust or control this mechanism.

In simple terms, a universe based on pure chance decrees that a coin toss has equal possibility of turning up heads or tails. However, a deterministic universe dictates that once the coin is tossed, its final state is *already decided* based on its trajectory and spin and the laws of physics. (Some would even go so far as to say the outcome is decided before the coin is tossed, because *the way it will be thrown* has been predetermined.)

Given these well entrenched, deterministic beliefs about the universe and the way we fit into it, it is easy to see how even our lives have been regarded as largely predetermined. For those who have experienced such phenomena, peering into the future has been regarded as a way of revealing events or outcomes that are unavoidable. Applied to the case of Dr John Demartini's vision, it would be assumed that he had a premonition of a career that had already been determined, and was fated to happen regardless of his actions.

However, the advent of quantum physics in the early twentieth century changed everything. By casting doubt on many Newtonian Laws, discoveries in quantum mechanics also put determinism under the spotlight. The universe began to look less like a machine, controlled by simple physical laws and tracking toward a series of inevitable outcomes. How can a universe — and everything in it — be predetermined when actions and reactions can happen instantaneously across distance or through time, or when the simple act of observing an event can affect its outcome?

This change of thinking meant a necessary rethink of the concept of the future and how we interact with it. The concept of a *probabilistic universe* emerged, where multiple outcomes are possible based on the predictable patterns of cause and effect, coupled with the impact of personal choices and actions. In the probabilistic universe, a tossed coin may be falling to its inevitable landing place ... but what happens if you willingly choose to flick it again, mid-flight?

As a young man, John Demartini was inherently strong-minded, intelligent, and unconditionally supported by his family. These factors may very well have determined that his future would always be one of success and inspiration. However, it was his personal will that took him first to the depths of personal experience and then to the heights. In the end he was responsible for creating the life promised by his vision in Hawaii. It was John himself who continued after Paul Bragg left. It was John Demartini who took a probable future — a vision of greatness — and made it a reality.

13

The Chosen One
Battagram KP, Pakistan

8:52am, 8 October 2005

Ihsan crouched low on the uneven path, his fingers grasping at the air around him in a vain attempt to stay upright. His body reverberated with the deep rumble of the earth and nausea rose from his gut. His sole focus became survival.

The ground shook, lurched and dropped violently. It felt almost as if the Earth was trying to throw him and all that he held dear from its surface. This is Doomsday, he thought. The ground is going to open up and swallow me.

One by one, he watched in horror as the houses on the ridge opposite exploded into clouds of silver rubble. In the valley below, the town of Battagram, his town, dissolved into ruins.

It was only three days since Ihsan had been elected into office but this, he knew, was the moment he had been waiting for all of his life.

Ihsan was raised in a simple hut, in the village of Ajmera on the outskirts of Battagram. His childhood had been a tough and lonely struggle of subsistence. In Pakistan the average wage was less than US$500 a year — and the area of Battagram was particularly underprivileged.

Despite an inevitable sense of hopelessness in his upbringing, Ihsan always felt he was destined for some kind of greatness. This sentiment had been echoed in his mother's dying words, "One day, son, you are going to be somebody. Like a king," she had whispered to him. So, when Ihsan was awarded a United States Green Card at the age of 18, he did not look back.

Ihsan landed in the USA in 1977 — a penniless but determined nineteen-year-old. By 1984, he had become a United States citizen. By 1987, he had a political science degree from Northern Illinois University. But, somehow, Ihsan's American Dream had become a dreary reality. By the mid-1980s, he was living in Washington DC, alone and lonely. He had long ago lost touch with his family back in Pakistan who, by now, assumed he was dead. After a brief stint as a security guard, Ihsan was scraping out a living as a taxi driver — often forced to sleep in his cab. Ihsan thought taxi driving was the worst job in the world and he often contemplated working himself to the point of heart attack, just so people would know the hardship he had suffered.

However, through these long, dark years, Ihsan's indomitable spirit was buoyed by two, delicate threads of hope — two flickers of light in his otherwise dreary existence. The first was a fortune cookie prediction — a crumpled piece of paper Ihsan carried in his wallet that proclaimed, *Among winners, you are the chosen one.* The second was the purchase of his weekly lottery ticket — a habit he had adopted after a profound dream.

The dream had come so long ago that Ihsan couldn't remember exactly when, but the details of the vision itself would never leave his memory. As it began, he had found himself in a beautiful place filled with loveliness, light and exquisite gems. "So many beautiful things, like diamonds and rubies," Ihsan would explain to those curious enough to ask.

The dream had then morphed, as dreams often do, and Ihsan found himself in a crowded room, speaking to an overwhelming mass of people. Then the numbers came to him, as clear as crystal: 246 1725 31.

The vision had come only once but Ihsan had paid it the attention it was due. For 10 years, maybe 12, he had purchased his personal slice of hope in the District of Colombia lottery and, every week, his ticket would be marked in his regular pattern: 2, 4, 6, 17, 25 and Powerball 31.

Wednesday, 21 November 2001, dawned just like any other for Ihsan Khan. It was the day before Thanksgiving and for 12 hours he had repeated the tedious drill of shuffling party-goers and out-of-towners around the streets of Washington D.C. But this day was destined to be different to any other for two, simple reasons. Firstly, Powerball was running a special $55 million jackpot — the largest prize pool in the history of the DC Lottery. Secondly, the balls that bounced out of the chute that night were 2, 4, 6, 17, 25 and Powerball 31.

After 20 years as a struggling taxi driver, and more than a decade of weekly lottery purchases, Ihsan Khan was a sudden and spectacular multi-millionaire.

From that night forward, Ihsan set about creating a new life for himself. He completed one last taxi ride, for free, before claiming his prize-money. He then purchased his dream car, a Mercedes-Benz 600, and bought two million-dollar mansions — one in Virginia and one in Islamabad.

But Ihsan's personal experience with struggle and his long-standing kinship with poverty remained powerful influences. Before long, he was searching for benevolent outlets for this new found fortune. "It's not about piling up money and forgetting others," he would explain. "We all have an obligation to help those less fortunate." Within a few years, Ihsan had decided to return to his home town of Battagram where, with his great wealth, he felt he could affect real and positive change.

It was the political scene of his local area that disturbed Ihsan the most on his return. Arriving back in Pakistan in 2005, at the age of forty-seven, he was confronted by overt corruption and nepotism in the local political arena. For 45 years, Battagram had been ruled by one local family and, to Ihsan, it seemed clear that public service was not their main motivation. Ihsan had come home to create positive change and, now, he saw how it needed to be done.

In late September 2005, just two weeks before the election, Ihsan had commenced his campaign for Nazim, mayor, of Battagram. Ihsan purchased advertising and marketing, and campaigned furiously for the position. His opposition put up a tough fight, publicly denouncing him as "American Dollar Man" or "Lottery Man", and accusing him of buying votes. But, in the end, the people of Battagram decided that Ihsan might just be the right man to lead them and, on October 5, 2005, he was elected as the new Nazim of Battagram. He wasted no time. Disgusted with the corruption he had seen at play, Ihsan immediately fired the police chief and several other crooked officials.

That had been three days ago.

As suddenly as it began, the intense jolting of the earth subsided. Ihsan struggled slowly to his feet and, for a brief second, all was still in the valley around him. The hillside sat scarred and expectant as graceful clouds of dust spiralled gently into the air. A sharp smell of disturbed spruce tickled at Ihsan's nose. The only sound was the soft shuffle of pebbles coming to rest on the mountain path.

Then, drifting up the valley on the gentle breeze, the noise of destruction arrived. Faintly, yet distinctly, Ihsan could hear the manic barking of feral dogs, the baying of donkeys, and the shrill screams of human suffering. Battagram, he knew, must be lying in ruins and only Allah knew how many lives had been lost.

Without delay, Ihsan sprang into action and began the long walk back to town. He was Nazim of Battagram and his people would be looking to him to help rebuild their lives. They needed his leadership and his direction. They needed his decisiveness and his support. But, more than that, Ihsan knew, right now the impoverished people of Battagram needed his money.

Khan rushed into the town and helped pull survivors from the rubble. Within hours, he paid to get the most seriously injured to regional hospitals, using a make-shift ambulance service. He cleaned out the local pharmacies, and covered the bill for all the medical supplies dispensed by these stores immediately after the quake.

Once the emergency medical situation had been taken care of, Khan turned his attention to helping protect and provide for the thousands of survivors in his electorate. He bought 150 tents for homeless families and allowed them to camp on his land, and he established a fund to help villagers rebuild their demolished homes. In all, it is estimated that Khan spent US$300,000 of his own funds on housing, medical equipment, tin roofing and other shelter.

The earthquake, with a moment magnitude of 7.6Mw, decimated the Khyber Pakhtunkhwa region of Pakistan. It would eventually claim more than 73,000 lives across the region — 4500 in Battagram alone. In December 2005, just two months after the quake, Khan's story featured in Time magazine and his incredible tale was shared with the world.[22]

Ihsan Khan is no longer the Nazim of Battagram, but his legacy lives on. He will long be remembered as the poor man who dreamt of the winning lottery numbers and then, in an incredible twist of fate, used his wealth to save thousands of lives. His mother's prophecy was fulfilled — Ihsan Khan did grow up to be 'somebody' in his region of Battagram — like a great and benevolent king.

The how, what and why of psi: Psychics and the lottery

One concept that has plagued supporters of psi in recent decades is the idea that those who are psychic would surely use their 'special' skill to win the lottery. It is a fair argument, assuming that psi information is somehow 'on tap' or that recipients have control over what they receive, and when.

Sometimes, people who receive the numbers through psi do win the lottery. Apart from Ihsan Khan in the late 1980s, in Florida, in 1998, Janine Cox amazed her friends and colleagues with her unprecedented winning streak in the State's Lotteries. Over a 33-day period, Cox won moderate sums of money 28 times in a row. Her secret? Each night she would dream of the next day's winning numbers.

According to an intriguing email Cox received from the Florida State Lottery, neither she nor Ihsan Khan are alone. The email, sent by a State Lottery employee named Rebecca, admitted to Cox that a number of prior lottery winners also claimed to have received their winning numbers in dreams.[23]

These stories hint at the fact that psi information can be used to win the lottery. However, these appear to be incredibly rare cases and, for most lottery players, winning the jackpot remains a matter of incredible luck. The question arises, therefore; what makes these cases different? If it is possible to foretell the winning numbers, why does it not happen all the time?

Although scientific understandings of psi are still rudimentary, those who work in this field have noted several consistent factors at play. Firstly, it appears that the human mind has trouble receiving and recalling numbers and letters. With a few notable exceptions, (such as US military remote viewer, Joe McMoneagle who was able to use psi to detect entire code names), the human brain finds it difficult to interpret anything too complex in the form of written language. Janine Cox, mentioned earlier, openly expressed her inability to recall longer number sequences from her dreams, and was most comfortable and accurate with the Pick3 lottery.

Studies in telepathy have revealed a similar pattern. Contrary to the age-old myth of 'reading people's minds' it appears that exact thoughts are not able to be accessed through psi. Rather, it is intentions, emotions or a general 'state of mind' that are most easily received and interpreted.

This apparent disconnect between left-brain processes, such as language and analysis, and the intuitive flow of psi information has been evident in other research areas. Studies as far back as the 1940s have shown that the brain can have trouble placing shapes and objects spatially, particularly when dealing with recurring shapes or patterns. For instance, when viewed remotely (ie. viewed across distance using only psi abilities), a row of windows may be interpreted as groups of horizontal and vertical lines. The specific elements of the window frames are received and acknowledged; however, the brain has trouble placing these elements together to form a square. Engineer and parapsychologist, René Wallcollier, called this phenomenon *parallelism*. Ingo Swann, a professional remote viewer and psi educator, refers to it as *lack of fusion*.

These early discoveries go some way to explaining what can be interpreted via psi and why some information is harder to receive than others. However, there are other, more profound, elements to this human capability that we are yet to understand. Ihsan Khan was not just given access to a multi-million-dollar lottery win. His win enabled him to assist thousands of homeless and starving families. Janine Cox was given information that won her hundreds of dollars at a time. She did not 'receive' winning codes that could have won her millions. As outlined in Chapter 16 of this book, the researcher Russell Targ was able to successfully predict the rise and fall of the share market, except when his express purpose was to make money from the exercise.

As yet, we have no understanding of why a person's intent appears to play a role in the psi information they receive. The answer may become clearer as our scientific knowledge increases. Will psychology discover that part of the human brain governs psi information in direct correlation to the purity of intent? Or perhaps global consciousness, (as explained in Chapter 4), is also a global conscience — a united morality that regulates the psi information available at any one time, to any one person, in favour of a greater good.

14

Who is Dead in the White House?
Washington DC, USA

2 June 1854

Mary Ann sat alone in the warm shadows while, on the mantle, the steady tick-tick of the clock signalled the approach of midnight. These were the final moments of her fifty-fourth birthday. In her hand, a single sheet of parchment — a birthday gift — glowed faintly luminous in the lamplight. She stared into the distance as her fingers stroked the words that had been carefully inscribed onto the paper.

They spoke of a loving mother; weary and patient. In the dark of night, the woman sat near a fireplace nursing her restless infant.

Shuddering slightly, Mary Ann thought back to another evening, nearly 16 years earlier — the night she had first seen her vision. Her fifth son, John, was just six months old at the time and she had been comforting him in the early hours of the morning. As she sat by the fire cradling the restless infant, Mary Ann was suddenly overcome with a sense of horror about his future, his destiny. In a moment of desperation, she sent up a fervent prayer, asking to be shown the fate that awaited her young son. In reply, a premonition had washed over her with terrifying clarity.

Beside her, in the swirling flames of the fire, Mary Ann could see strange apparitions. Then her eyes became transfixed on her son's tiny hand, vulnerable and innocent. Within moments, she was consumed with a certainty that her child's hand would one day do something of terrible significance.

The poem she held now explained, in gentle phrases, the torment of that moment. And how, in the loneliness of the dark room, she had yearned for her infant to answer one question:

What force, what power is at your command,
For evil, or good? [24]

The premonition of that night was permanently etched into Mary Ann's memory and she often spoke of the experience with her youngest daughter, Asia. Then this year, 1854, as her son turned 16, the premonition had returned as a terrifying dream. Today, Asia, with love and concern, had immortalised the vision in a poem — a birthday gift for her mother.

The poem was exquisitely presented, flowing down the page in Asia's careful calligraphy. But the verses held no beauty – they were dark and menacing. They spoke of blood and vengeance; of patriotism and country.

Mary Ann let the parchment fall to her lap and sighed deeply. Whatever terrible fate awaited her son, she sensed she was powerless to stop it. She clasped her hands softly beneath her chin and began to pray for her safety and salvation ... and that of her beloved boy, John Wilkes Booth.

******

12 April 1865

Of all the rooms in the Executive Mansion, the library was Abraham's favourite. It was here, on the south side of the second floor, that he would retreat at the end of the day for a few, precious moments of peace.

Elsewhere in the building, Abe was under constant demand from throngs of White House inhabitants. The halls were always teeming with people — aides requiring direction, journalists seeking information, generals sharing the latest troop movements or presidential pilgrims just hoping to catch a glimpse of his wiry frame. But here, in his private library, surrounded by his treasured books and eclectic furniture, Abe could finally shrug off the mantle of President and be husband, father and man. Here, he was simply Abraham Lincoln.

In recent days, Abe's need for isolation appeared more extreme than usual. Four years of civil war had worn his natural soberness into an almost-permanent melancholy. In the past, Abe had always relied on humour to lift a gloomy mood but lately he seemed unable to call upon his usual irrepressible wit. Even the surrender of the Confederate leader, General Lee, had failed to lift his mood.

This lack of spirit was not lost on those nearest to him — his wife, Mary, and his close friend and unofficial bodyguard, Ward 'Hill' Lamon.

Tonight, Abe's mood was particularly bleak and sombre. As was so often the case, he had not been able to retire to the library until late evening. When he did, both Mary and Hill were waiting for him. Mary was the first to voice her concerns. A forthright and curious woman, she questioned Abe insistently about his deep frown and pensive mood until, eventually, he relented. He began to ponder on the subject of dreams.

"It seems strange how much there is in the Bible about dreams," he began. "There are, I think, some sixteen chapters in the Old Testament and four or five in the New in which dreams are mentioned. And many other passages scattered throughout refer to visions. If we believe the Bible, we must accept the fact that in the old days God and His angels came to men in their sleep and made themselves known in dreams."[25]

As Abe spoke, Mary and Hill listened in quiet concern. Lincoln was known as a man with a sharp intellect and logical nature, but those close to him were also aware of his deep, mystical side. Abe regarded the sixth sense as a valuable resource of the common folk and often held it in higher regard than knowledge. Whereas others may have regarded this as odd or 'supernatural', Abe was convinced that it was a completely natural phenomenon. Everything in nature was perfect, he reasoned, therefore these insights must be a natural expression of the almighty intelligence that governed the universe.

Over time, Abe had learned to trust his own mystical insight. Throughout his presidency, he often bemused those around him with his uncanny insights and premonitions, and his dreams were known to be deeply symbolic. However, despite his respect for visions and premonitions, Abe always approached these insights with a healthy dose of pragmatism — especially if he was the subject of such a vision.

From childhood, Abe had a sense that he would be struck down suddenly after reaching lofty heights, and many of the mystics in his private circle (the mediums and seers that often visited the White House) had warned him of a possible assassination. However, Abe paid little attention to these warnings and chose instead to maintain a stoic optimism that good would prevail and he would remain safe.

Even his vision in November 1860 — the night he was first elected — had failed to dim his belief. After a long night of celebration, Abe returned to his home in Springfield and slumped, exhausted, onto a couch in his bed chamber. By chance, he caught his reflection in a looking glass and the apparition that stared back at him was both ominous and mysterious. There in the polished glass was not one reflection but two — the face of the newly elected President, healthy and vibrant and another version of the same face, shimmering and ghostly pale. The vision had worried Abe a little but the meaning seemed clear — to him and to Mary.

Abe was certain he would be elected twice to the presidency, but not live to see the end of his second term.

Despite these shadowy premonitions and his recent re-election, Abe refused to succumb to fear. He lived each day with calm conviction and was generally philosophical about his future. For this reason, Abe's statement about dreams, on that April evening, left both Mary and Hill deeply troubled. Whatever Abe was alluding to, it had left him shaken and Mary was determined to find out why. She pressed him for more. "You look dreadfully solemn. Do you believe in dreams?" she asked.

"I can't say that I do." Abe was hesitant with his answer. As troubled as he was by his thoughts, he was not keen to burden his wife with them. But Mary was not to be denied. As the conversation continued, she peppered Abe with questions and strongly urged him to reveal his thoughts. Eventually, with a deep sigh and a melancholy frown, Abe relented.

"About ten days ago, I retired very late," he began. His words were steady and deliberate. "I could not have been long in bed when I fell into a slumber, for I was weary. I soon began to dream."

Mary and Hill listened intently as Abe described the scene that had come to him while he slept. He told them of a death-like stillness that cocooned him in his bed, and the gentle sobbing that slowly filtered into his awareness. Several people were weeping, but Abe was unable to tell who they were, or where they were located. Rising slowly from his bed, Abe made his way through the various rooms of the White House. The pitiful sobbing filled the halls of the mansion, but the source of the crying remained unclear. Not a living soul was in sight — just the empty rooms, and the mysterious weeping.

In the dream Abe made his way to the East Room, the grand ballroom on the ground floor. What he saw there shocked him to his core. Around the room, crowds of people were gathered, many of them weeping openly and staring vacantly. In the centre of the space, guarded by a handful of soldiers, Abe saw a corpse wrapped in funeral robes resting on an ornate catafalque. But the face of the corpse was covered — the identity of the deceased was a mystery.

Mary and Hill listened with increasing horror. Abe's face was pale and his expression gloomy, but his voice remained steady. "I demanded to know — who is dead in the White House?" Abe paused for the briefest of moments and the shock of the dream flooded across his face. Then, slowly, calmly, Abraham Lincoln repeated the soldier's response.

"It is the President," he said. "He was killed by an assassin."

******

14 April 1865

It was the finest celebration Julia had ever seen. She had arrived the previous afternoon on the Mary Martin, a government dispatch boat, and was astonished by the colour, noise and jubilation that greeted her. For four, long years the country had endured a bloody civil war and now, finally, the Confederate surrender had been secured. General Lee was in custody. The South had capitulated. The war was over and Washington D.C. was in a joyous uproar.

Even Mother Nature had been congratulatory — the sun shone brilliantly as the boat made its way up the Potomac River. As they pulled into the docks, a gust of wind unfurled the flag posted at the landing as if to announce to the jubilant crowd that all the stars were, indeed, united again.

Of course, the cheers and salutes of the crowd had not been directed at Julia; they were for her husband, General Ulysses Grant, revered leader of the Union Army. The morning papers were full of news of their arrival and the ongoing festivities. "The illumination of the city this evening is general and brilliant, utterly beyond anything ever before attempted here, and has drawn thousands upon thousands of persons upon the streets," read the New York Times. "Pennsylvania-avenue is a line of light from First street to Twenty-second-street, a distance of nearly two miles, there being but very few houses on either side in that whole extent which are not illuminated."[26]

Julia had seen the illumination. The day of her arrival, after dark, she had left Willard's Hotel with her husband to ride through the streets. All over the city, houses and buildings were lit up with candles and lamps and adorned with flags and bunting. Thousands of people were gathered to witness this incredible light show and they shouted messages of thanks and congratulations to General Grant as he rode by.

Julia loved pageantry and she was immensely proud of her husband. To see the whole of Washington DC in celebration, to know that her husband was the cause of such jubilation, was a dream come true. Everyone wanted to talk to her, everyone wanted to be seen with her, and the General, her General, was the toast of the town.

So, Julia could not understand why she wanted to leave.

The feeling had come upon her the moment she awoke that morning. As soon as the General opened his eyes, Julia had begged him to leave Washington immediately. He had replied that he wished he could, but that President Lincoln had requested a meeting with him. Perhaps in the evening, he had suggested. The feeling had only intensified throughout the day and, by midday, when a message arrived from Mary Lincoln, Julia could think of little else.

Mrs Lincoln was requesting that she and the General attend Ford's Theater that night, to sit with them in the President's own box. It was a supreme honour but Julia turned it down immediately. Her yearning for home was uncontrollable — she referred to the feeling as 'freak' — and she could not tolerate staying in Washington.

As soon as she had declined Mrs Lincoln's invitation, Julia sent a message to her husband. She would not attend the theatre. She would not stay in Washington a day longer. She simply must go home. Throughout the afternoon, several officers stopped by to pay their respects, and Julia sent each of them to General Grant to reinforce her request.

Eventually, the General conceded. In the mid-afternoon Julia finally received word to pack her belongings — they would travel on the late afternoon train.

When the Grants eventually left the noisy gaiety of the capital, Julia's relief was palpable. She was unable to explain her strange behaviour or the irresistible urge that had overtaken her. All she knew was that there was nothing sweeter than the sound she heard now — the sweet clacking of the wheels on the railroad track. On her way home to Burlington, with her beloved husband by her side, Julia could finally relax.

General Grant did not make it home that night. By the time he and his wife, Julia, arrived in Philadelphia, several telegraph messages were waiting for him with the tragic news. After Grant's departure, the President had attended Ford's Theater as planned. There, in his private box, he had been shot by a lone assassin. By early morning, Abraham Lincoln was dead and, just as his eerie dream had predicted, a nation was thrown into mourning.

As well as targeting Abraham Lincoln, it was later discovered that the murderous plot had included shooting several other senior government officials. One bullet remained unused because its intended target was not in the theatre that night. That bullet had been meant for Julia's husband, General Ulysses Grant. Julia's inexplicable urge to leave Washington had saved her husband's life.

Lincoln's killer would later be identified as a young, well-to-do Confederate patriot — a vehement supporter of the South. This assassin, whose hand pulled the trigger and tragically changed history, was John Wilkes Booth.

Soon after Lincoln's assassination, Julia Grant's young daughter Nellie appeared to have a premonition of living in the White House. She spoke of living in "a great, great house ... like the Capitol in Washington."[27] Nellie's intuition proved to be correct. On 4 March 1869, General Grant became President Ulysses Grant, the 18th President of the United States of America.

Precognition: A matter of time

Precognition is used to describe the experience of receiving information about a future event. The term includes premonition (vision or knowledge of a future event) and presentiment (an unconscious emotional response triggered by a future event).

For centuries, the idea of peering into the future was regarded as utter nonsense. It was assumed that time was completely linear and flowed in only one direction; from the past towards the future. However, in March 1955, Einstein boldly wrote in a personal letter "the distinction between past, present and future is only a stubbornly persistent illusion". This statement signalled the emergence of a new understanding about the nature of time.

Through the work of physicists such as David Bohm and the controversial Julian Barbour, it is becoming apparent that human understanding of time is misguided and largely incomplete. It can be said that what we perceive as time is actually our response to irreversible physical phenomena such as chemical reactions, ageing and the ticking of a clock. However, there are many effects in the universe that are not time-indicative, such as the melting and freezing of water and the laws of mechanics when there is no friction (as in a swinging pendulum). It is entirely possible that our experience of psi relies on some such phenomenon — one that sits outside the discernible passage of time.

In the laboratory, meta-analysis has revealed compelling evidence for precognition, (with odds against chance of 10 million billion billion to one), much of which has been successfully replicated.[28] In recent years, Daryl Bem's nine-year study into precognition suggests that humans can, and do, have a very real reaction to future stimuli.[29] These results shatter all impressions of a one-way flow of time, and provide tantalising evidence that people can, in fact, foretell the near future in a clinical environment.

It is interesting to note that people are more inclined to have precognitions if the future event is highly emotive. For instance, Dean Radin discovered that percipients would display a physiological response a few seconds before being shown a violent or erotic picture, however no such response would occur if the picture was neutral.[30] It might reasonably be concluded, therefore, that the assassination of Abraham Lincoln in 1865 could trigger several precognitions. It is entirely possible that the intense shock and sadness of a grieving nation reverberated through time and caused premonitions in Lincoln and the mother of his killer, and a strong presentiment in the wife of an intended victim.

15

"I Saw Her Too!"
Kangchenjunga, The Himalaya

Lou picked his way gingerly over the rutted ground as night wrapped its first tentative fingers around him. To his left, Kangchenjunga rose like a sentinel above the valley, the sacred summit almost hidden from sight in the deepening twilight. Kangchenjunga: The Five Treasure Houses of the Snows — the third tallest mountain on Earth.

As with all the major campaigns, the Kangchenjunga expedition had been years in the planning, but it had presented some unique complications. The permit to ascend from Sikkim — the Indian side of the mountain — had only been granted after US Senator, Ted Kennedy, had kindly interceded on Lou's behalf. More recently, his planning time had been cut in half due to a location swap with a Russian team, and the deteriorating political situation between India and Nepal had thrown their supply chain into complete disarray.

But Lou Whittaker was not a quitter. Known for his rare blend of determination, warmth and exquisite leadership, he led his team, many of them tired and ill, to set up base camp on the north side of the mountain. Finally, they were here, in April 1989, poised to be the first American team to reach the summit of Kangchenjunga.

In the twilight Lou stood at the entrance to his tent and turned to watch the dark shadows swallow the mountain. He knew that the true challenge was yet to come. Stooping deeply, he folded his lofty frame through the flap and went inside.

The sensation was upon him in an instant. She was here again, just as she was every night. Lou smiled softly as the now-familiar presence washed over him. He gently sealed the flap against the cold night air and relaxed in the knowledge that all was well.

******

It had been an amazing trek for Ingrid Whittaker and her group of nine. The spring weather had been kind and the Kangchenjunga region had seemed eager to impress the trekkers with its spectacular beauty. Their journey had taken them past towering oak trees, forests of vibrant rhododendrons, meadows of flowering alpine shrubs, and villages bustling with healthy, smiling locals. And throughout, in the distance, Kangchenjunga beckoned them on, dazzling them in its silver-blue finery.

The hikers were in high spirits so, when Ingrid suggested that they miss their last resting stage and press on to the base camp, it didn't take much to persuade them. For this group, base camp was the pinnacle of their trek; for Ingrid it also meant a long-awaited reunion with her husband, Lou. Fuelled on by enthusiasm, the group eagerly devoured the distance to base camp and climbed from 3600 metres to 4900 metres in one day.

The sickness claimed Ingrid before they arrived. Altitude sickness.

Ingrid was a highly experienced climber and she knew the symptoms. Her body was struggling to adjust to less oxygen and lower air pressure and, as their destination grew nearer, her head began to throb. There would be no celebration; no joyous reunion. As she arrived at base camp, exhausted and nauseous, Ingrid instantly climbed into Lou's tent and fell onto the 'bed'.

The headache was unrelenting.

For the next few days, Ingrid lay almost motionless in the tent consumed by the excruciating pain and persistent nausea. At night, Lou was next to her, soothing her, but throughout the day he was out climbing and preparing for the big ascent. It was during these absences that Ingrid became aware of another comforting presence, watching over her as she lay there alone.

Most of the time, Ingrid was simply aware of the woman; a hovering presence; a sense of comfort. But at times Ingrid's awareness would become more acute, and the enigmatic woman would come into view. She was a local, dressed in the headscarf and long dress of the Himalaya. She did not appear to Ingrid in solid form, but as a shadowy figure. She was ethereal and two-dimensional.

As the days past and Ingrid battled through her illness, her rational mind fought to explain this mysterious apparition — at times, Ingrid was sure that she was delusional and that she was going to die. Still, the local woman watched on. Occasionally, she would send silent messages of comfort. At other times, she would gently help Ingrid to roll over or simply lay formless hands on Ingrid's forehead as if to ease the pain.

On the fourth day, Ingrid finally staggered out of the tent and back down the mountain. As she descended, her headache finally abated and she was able to continue to guide her trekking group through the Himalaya. Meanwhile Lou and his expedition turned their full attention to the beckoning summit of Kangchenjunga.

******

It was a happy day in June 1989 when the couple were finally reunited in the United States. Lou was jubilant after successfully leading his expedition to the summit of Kangchenjunga, and he and Ingrid celebrated together. They reflected on the joys and challenges of their latest trip but, even in the safety of her own home, and in the company of her beloved husband, Ingrid found it difficult to talk to Lou about what she had witnessed as she lay ill on the mountainside.

It was some time before she managed to open up to Lou. She was sure that her 'vision' was a hallucination and that she would be met with scepticism or disbelief. Eventually, cautiously, she told him of the comforting presence and the kindly apparition that had nursed her while she lay alone in the tent on Kangchenjunga. Lou's reply was instantaneous and astonishing.

"I saw her too!" he replied with amazement. Lou recalled the profound presence he had felt in his tent each evening; the regular visitations of a kindly, middle-aged woman. "While we were separated she was in my tent every night, comforting me and letting me know that everything was going to be ok," he explained.

After 40 years of experience, Lou Whittaker has become one of America's most respected mountaineers. Today, he is regarded as a legend on his home 'turf' of Mount Rainier, Washington, USA where he and Ingrid own a mountain lodge. Both Lou and Ingrid have undertaken many expeditions since Kangchenjunga, but neither has ever had such a profound mystical experience again. However, they are both adamant that what they witnessed was real, and they remain grateful to the kind apparition that watched over them both — the "gift from the gods of the Five Treasure Houses of the Snows".[31]

The science of spirit: Psi or survival?

Over the last century, as a growing number of scientists have begun to dismantle our previous assumptions about the laws of physics, many 'mystical' experiences have come under the spotlight. One of the unexpected dilemmas arising from our new, quantum reality is determining where the ancient idea of 'spirit' fits into the picture.

Since the beginning of time, millions of people have shared stories of visitations from deceased (discarnate) beings and in the last century, researchers have attempted to better understand this phenomenon. The general consensus (among those who have experienced some form of spirit communication) is that this phenomenon is indicative of the survival of consciousness — that is, life after death. However, with new scientific understandings of psi and how it appears to work, this concept has been put into question.

Evidence suggests that psi information can be obtained through time (both past and future) and over long distances. Therefore, these discarnate visitations could be the result of consciousness surviving death or they could be simply a psi experience reaching through time and space. With that understanding in mind, what Lou and Ingrid experienced on the slopes of Kangchenjunga (and what thousands of others experience every year) could be any of the following:

- Remote viewing: Were both Lou and Ingrid receiving psi information about someone who was alive, and living in the proximity of Kangchenjunga?
- Telepathy: Was Ingrid's vision simply a hallucination that Lou connected with telepathically, both prior to and after the event?

- Discarnate being: Did Lou and Ingrid experience the presence of a discarnate (deceased) local woman?

For the past decade The Windbridge Institute for Applied Research in Human Potential has been researching the possibility of consciousness survival. In that time, their studies have produced significant evidence that accurate information can be received about discarnate beings (deceased people), their families and their experiences — apparently from the deceased individuals themselves.

Scientific research into consciousness survival is still in its infancy but, at this stage, it does appear that experiences with spirit (like the one that occurred on the side of Kangchenjunga) do differ slightly from other psi experiences. Preliminary studies have shown that trained and experienced participants are able to differentiate between a psi experience with a living source, and an interaction with a person who is deceased.[32] Why, exactly, this difference exists — how information is apparently received from deceased individuals and where the information comes from — is yet to be determined and is a matter for future research.

16

Jesse Couldn't Resist
Atlantic City NJ, USA

It was a pleasantly fresh day in Atlantic City in the spring of 1906, and Jesse had come to enjoy a relaxing vacation. He held no stock at the moment and had taken the opportunity to rest while the market was steady.

Jesse had learned the terminology of Wall Street as a teenager — bull and bear — and the metaphor was as simple as it was menacing. A bull thrusts its horns up to attack and a bear swipes its paw down — the volatile stock market could go either way.

Lately it had not been Jesse Livermore's kind of market. It was bullish — steady, transparent and showing good indications for general business. Jesse, the 'Great Bear of Wall Street', had no interest in it.

The day had been as predictable as the market. Jesse and his friend had devoured the New York papers over breakfast, and had wasted a good portion of the morning watching the seagulls soar into the sky to drop defenceless clams onto the beach below then swoop down to devour the smashed morsels. When they tired of the avian entertainment, they headed along the Boardwalk to breathe in the salt air and take in the scenery.

As was their custom, prompted by pure curiosity, their feet trod an unconscious path into the local office of Harding Brothers, Jesse's stockbroker. The board that day showed an active and buoyant market — the sharks on Wall Street were riding high on a wave of optimism and unbridled greed. Jesse glanced at the numbers with barely concealed disinterest, and daydreamed while his friend began an animated monologue about the importance of holding moderate stock.

As Jesse's gaze flickered across the numbers, it alighted on Union Pacific.

Representing the largest railroad system in the United States, Union Pacific was a powerhouse on the stock market. Only 10 years earlier, the company had been sold for $110 million and, since then, had continued to thrive. Through the acquisition of Southern Pacific and the construction of the Western line, Union Pacific had grown to dominate rail transport throughout the mid-West and into the vital San Francisco port, in California. It was an immovable monolith; a profitable certainty.

Jesse's eyes scanned the figures. I've got to sell that. The urge inside him was both instant and irrepressible. He couldn't think of a rational reason to sell. All logic dictated that Union Pacific was solid. It was expanding. Selling stock in that company was tantamount to insanity.

I've got to sell. Jesse couldn't resist the persistent thought. On the board, the numbers had disappeared into a dark haze and Jesse's friend had stopped his patter to stare at him intently. "Are you going to sleep?" he asked.

"No," replied Jesse. "What I'm going to do is sell Union Pacific stock."

Almost automatically, Jesse walked to a nearby table, reached for a blank order pad and began to fill it out. He didn't own any shares, but that didn't matter. His intention was to sell 'short' — a practice Jesse had become renowned for. He would instruct Harding Brothers to sell Union Pacific on his behalf and pocket the proceeds, on the understanding that he would buy the shares back from the broker later, at market value. He was effectively gambling on the stock price dropping. It was a risky move at best. It seemed a foolhardy one in a raging bull market. He wrote the ticket for 1000 shares.

The manager was smiling as Jesse approached him with the order, but his beam faded into a confused frown as he read the details. "Is this right?" he asked. Jesse replied with a cool stare and the manager scurried away, barely daring to dream of the profit he was about to make.

Jesse's friend pounced on him with a desperate curiosity. "What are you doing?" he whispered.

"I'm selling a thousand UP," Jesse replied.

"What?"

Incredulous, Jesse's friend grabbed him by the arm and dragged him out of the broker's office. Union Pacific was one of his pets but if Jesse Livermore was making a move then there was something amiss, and he needed to be a part of it. "Why in the blazes are you selling?"

Jesse faced his friend's overt excitement with sombre honesty, "I don't know," he replied, "I just know something is going to happen, and I want to sell that stock ... in fact I'm going to let them have another thousand!" He strolled back inside to write the order for another 1000 shares. And then another.

Three thousand shares 'short' of Union Pacific, the biggest bull in a roaring market. Jesse felt calm; reassured, but it was too much for his friend. Grabbing Jesse firmly by the arm, he whisked him out of the office again and into the New Jersey air. "You're crazy," he hissed. "Stark raving crazy!"

The next day, the general market rose higher, but a quiet certainty had settled over Jesse. He knew he was right to sell Union Pacific, and he was prepared to be patient. By that afternoon, the persistent urge had returned. Jesse made his way to Harding Brothers and sold another 2000 shares.

He'd reached his limit. Unable to sell anymore at the local Harding Brothers, and feeling a need to be back in the action, Jesse cut his vacation short and headed back to New York that evening.

The news came the very next day. It trickled through the streets of New York, and flowed into the salons and billiard halls. By midday, Wall Street was alive with the news; the paper boys were battling for supremacy; their cries becoming increasing sensational. San Francisco had been hit by a violent earthquake, and the greatest port on the West Coast had been reduced to a pile of burning rubble.

The market didn't respond immediately. Blinded by optimism and isolated from the terrible devastation, Wall Street continued to rally. But it was only a matter of time, and Jesse backed his uncanny intuition even further, selling another 10,000 Union Pacific shares short.

The next day, he cleaned up. The reality of San Francisco in ruins finally began to hit home. Union Pacific, the greatest transport company in the West, had been left without its headquarters and much of its infrastructure. The stock price plummeted as investors scrambled to insulate themselves from the long, hard road of an expensive rebuild. Jesse, acting on nothing more than an uncanny intuitive hunch, walked away with a total profit of $250,000 — healthy earnings for three days' work.

For the next 20 years, Jesse Livermore continued to dominate the US stock market, earning the nickname "the Boy Plunger". A year after his success with Union Pacific he intuitively predicted the stock market panic of 1907, netting a profit of $3 million. But it is his premonition of the 1929 Wall Street Crash for which he is most famous. Following his uncanny hunches, and selling short, Jesse earned the grand sum of $100 million, while most around him folded into bankruptcy.

Jesse never understood his hunches, but he never doubted them. Throughout his career, he continued to trust his precognition and openly regretted the times he ignored his instincts in favour of logic or reason. Sadly, he eventually succumbed to deep depression and over-spending, taking his own life in 1940. But even today, his legend lives on and he is still regarded as one of the most uncanny and most intuitive traders Wall Street has ever seen.

Corporate intuition: The inside knowledge

In recent years, the value of intuition has been openly praised in the corporate world. Richard Branson relies on it, Steve Jobs openly encouraged it and Estée Lauder built an entire perfume empire on it. (Two of her best sellers are called "Knowing" and "Intuition" — a reference to her inner mentor.)

But, as interesting as these anecdotal references may be, it is science that has provided the most compelling evidence for a sixth sense, and how it may be the most powerful, most profitable business tool around.

In 1982, NASA physicist and father of the modern laser, Russell Targ, conducted a controlled experiment on the possibility of using psi perception to make money on the stock market. He gathered a small team together: a businessman, a stockbroker, a willing investor and a well trained and experienced 'remote viewer', or clairvoyant. Over nine weeks, in late 1982, his team played the December Silver market, investing and withdrawing their funds based on the premonition of the team's remote viewer.[33]

The results were astounding. For over two months, they successfully forecasted every weekly movement of December Silver and walked away from the trial with a healthy profit of $120,000. Their enterprise was later featured on the first page of the Wall Street Journal and, in 1983, a documentary was made about it for the BBC Horizon series.[34]

These results were successfully replicated in 2013 by a professor and his students at the University of Colorado.[35] Using a strict protocol and the combined predictions of all participants, the group managed to predict the movements of the Dow Jones Index, seven times in a row. In just two weeks, their initial investment of $10,000 was converted into a healthy $26,000 (and would have been more if they had sold all shares at the immediate conclusion of the experiment).

17

Angry Mist and Thunderous Noise
Giraween NSW, Australia

"Thanks everyone. That's all for today," Brendan announced.

Kim gathered her script, empty lunchbox and water bottle and flung them haphazardly into her backpack. Musical theatre was her greatest joy — she never felt more alive than when singing in front of an audience — but even she found the last few rehearsals before show time a little dull and strained. By now, all the lines were habitual, all the choreography was committed to muscle memory and there was a growing sense of eagerness to 'just get to the performance'.

Coupled with that was the December heat. The annual showcase was an end-of-year performance so the final few rehearsals were always conducted in the height of the Australian summer. In a warehouse-type studio, with no air-conditioning and limited airflow, the heat of 30 dancing bodies could be stifling.

Today had been particularly suffocating. As the afternoon progressed, the humidity had risen and a blanket of damp heat had settled over north-west Sydney. Kim had not seen the sky since morning but as the rehearsal came to an end she could sense the menacing tension of a storm approaching. Thank God. The cool change was always welcome in summer.

Kim stood back as the ensemble of weary performers made their way down the narrow corridor to the studio exit. Most of the troupe were children — emerging 'triple threats' studying at Brendan's performing arts school — so the exit was crowded with parents, older siblings and other designated drivers. There was no rush. Kim had arrived early and parked her car at the rear of the carpark, near the studio entrance. Even if she had left at the front of the pack, her vehicle was sure to be blocked in the carpark until the others had left.

It was only as the last few stragglers waved their goodbyes that Kim reached into the front of her bag for her car keys. They weren't there. Frowning, she checked again. Nothing. She set her bag down on the ground and searched carefully through the front pocket again. Strange, she thought, I swear I put them in there.

Kim began emptying her hastily-filled backpack onto the corridor floor. One by one she checked the compartments and the hidden folds and wrinkles. Front pocket. Main pocket. Side pockets. Inside pouch and coin pocket.

There were only two keys — a plastic-coated car key and a simple house key — but the key chain was relatively bulky. Beads, baubles and dangling ornaments — a chain designed to be the perfect target for a fumbling hand in the depths of a well-used handbag. After a full investigation of her backpack, she checked the empty studio, but no keys.

There was only one logical explanation. "Someone must have accidentally taken my keys with them," she said to Brendan.

The studio was in the industrial suburb of Girraween, a 30-minute drive from Kim's home in Cherrybrook. So, she phoned her husband, Todd. "Honey. I am so sorry, but someone has taken my car keys home with them. I think the spare key is on the kitchen bench — can you please drive over with it?"

Todd was calm. "No worries," he replied. "I'll pop the kids in the car and be right there. Where did you say it was?"

The air was heavy with humidity and, in the distance, a faint rumble echoed across the sky. "It's on the bench top. It should be right next to you."

For several moments, Kim waited while Todd scoured the kitchen for the spare car key. Then she waited several more as he checked the living room, the entryway side table, the bedroom, under the family room furniture. By the time he had completed his fruitless search, it was 15 minutes since the last performer had left. Kim was keeping Brendan from his family. It was time to go.

"Oh, honey. Just come and get me. I'll leave my car here and we'll figure out who has my keys later." The first few spots of rain were drifting down as Kim hung up the phone and settled in for her half-hour wait.

Brendan refused to leave. It was not in his nature to lock up and go home while one of his patrons was still waiting at the studio. So, the pair stood together under the covered entryway trading witty jokes and watching the raindrops on the carpark outside.

When the hail arrived, it did so without warning; the raindrops suddenly became interspersed with bullets of ice. Then, within seconds, the rain disappeared completely and the sky erupted in a mass of frozen missiles.

The noise was deafening as hail hit the roof, the ground, the vehicles. Brendan turned to Kim with a rueful smile. "I hope you have insurance," he quipped lightly.

"Actually, we don't," Kim replied. "The bill came in last month but we haven't paid it yet."

Brendan was gone in an instant; dashing into the studio door at alarming speed. Within seconds, he had returned with a roll of discarded carpet draped heavily over his shoulder. Then, before Kim could comprehend what was happening, he ran into the hail and threw the thick protective covering over the entire length of her car.

Just as Brendan returned, soaked to the bone and bruised by the brutal pellets of ice, the hail turned larger, louder and more violent. Shards of ice the size of marbles pelted the ground at staggering speed. And then, the hail became bigger still. For the next few minutes time stood still and the world became an anarchy of giant hailstones, angry mist and thunderous noise.

Eventually, the fury of the storm subsided to a benign drizzle and within 10 minutes, Todd had arrived with their two wide-eyed and excited children. "We caught the edge of the storm," Todd explained. "But just as it started, the car in front of us stopped under a railway bridge. We were stuck behind them … but under shelter."

The wild storm was the main topic of conversation on the drive home, but it wasn't until they approached Cherrybrook that the full magnitude of the hail became apparent. Here, the streets were lined with shredded trees — branches hanging like severed limbs, trunks stripped of bark. On the roads, drivers were carefully manoeuvring their demolished cars — dented roofs, smashed windows — through the intersections.

Outside their home, Kim and Todd gaped at the piles of giant hail lying like snow drifts in the shadows. In their street verandah roofs were peppered with grapefruit-sized holes where hail had smashed through. This had been no ordinary storm. It had been devastating; dangerous.

The realisation hit Todd as he parked his car. "Oh my God. This car was parked outside — if we hadn't gone to get you, it would have been demolished," he exclaimed.

"Well, I would have been driving in it!" Kim gasped. "Right through the worst of it. I can't imagine what could have happened."

It was the first thing Kim saw as she entered the house. Sitting boldly on the kitchen bench, in plain view, was the spare key to her car. "It's right here," she turned to Todd. "Right here, where I said."

Todd shook his head in bewilderment. "I looked there. I looked everywhere. I moved everything," he replied. "I truly didn't see it," he exclaimed.

Kim shook her head and, muttering under her breath about "needing a woman to look for things," made her way into the lounge. Wearily, she opened the main zipper of her backpack, placed it down on the carpeted floor and glanced as the bag gently toppled over. The thud was almost inaudible, but the flash of silver and black was unmistakable. With a furrowed brow, Kim bent down and picked up the set of keys that had fallen from inside the backpack. Her keys; dangling cheerfully from the beads and baubles of her ornamental key chain.

From the Australian Bureau of Meteorology:

9 December 2007
Severe storm with giant hail hits NW Sydney
A severe thunderstorm crossed Sydney's western and northern suburbs around 4pm producing many reports of golf ball to tennis ball size hail... The largest confirmed hail size was 7cm at Blacktown ... with an unconfirmed report of 11cm hail at Cherrybrook. The damage bill exceeded $200 million dollars with more than 6000 calls for assistance received by the SES. The supercell is probably the most significant single thunderstorm event to impact on Sydney since the infamous hailstorm that struck the eastern suburbs in April 1999.

This is my story. The destruction that my family and I witnessed that afternoon was extraordinary. Thankfully, our home sustained only minor damage to the verandah roof but many in our home suburb of Cherrybrook were left with badly smashed roofs, windows and external appliances and fittings. Trees and gardens were destroyed in the icy onslaught. Power remained off for most of the evening as repairs were made to damaged substations and electrical lines.

But the greatest destruction was to the vehicles in the area. (Years on, the hail damage was still evident on many cars around our suburb). Some were lucky to have dented bodywork; other vehicles were completely destroyed. But Todd and I were spared any such financial harm. Both of our vehicles — one of which was uninsured at the time — escaped without any damage at all. One was blocked in under an overbridge during the worst of the storm, and the other was protected under a length of old carpet.

It was a very lucky break — but one that could only have occurred because the keys to my car mysteriously, yet genuinely, disappeared for a brief moment. For one hour of our lives, neither Todd nor I could locate (or see) the keys that would have allowed me to drive home that afternoon, into the eye of one of the most destructive hail storms in Sydney's history.

Psychokinesis: the new reality of subjective reality

One of the most pervasive assumptions of Newtonian science is that the world we perceive through our senses is 'reality', and our experience revolves around the absolute existence of the physical universe. Through our attention we are able to observe our environment and the observation is a one-way interaction — what is happening 'out there' flows into our minds.

From this perspective, the idea that the physical world can be influenced through psi is regarded as impossible and farcical. If the physical world is the basis of reality then there is no possibility that one's mind can bend spoons, transport objects or make items disappear. These must be simply magic tricks and illusions.

The concept that 'out there' is the basis of reality is deeply entrenched in our psyche and is regarded by most people as an irrefutable fact. It is this concept that underpins the entire concept of life and (apart from some Eastern philosophies) determines how people interact with the world around them. Therefore, many would be surprised to learn that this concept of reality is scientifically disputable. As physicist Bernard d'Espagnat wrote, "The doctrine that the world is made up of objects whose existence is independent of human consciousness turns out to be in conflict with quantum mechanics and with facts established by experiment".[36]

There is now a plethora of scientific evidence suggesting that mind-matter interaction is a 'dual-carriageway'. While we are observing the physical world, our observations can, and do, change what we have focused our attention (or intention) on. This includes elements of the physical universe. From experimental results, theories are emerging that point to a completely different view of what is real, and why it is real. The emergence of defining concepts, such the paradox of Schrödinger's Cat, and Bell's Theorem, have altered the course of physics and opened the door for a physical reality that is not necessarily static, permanent … or there at all.

In this new age of physics — an era of probability waves, consciousness, entanglement and 'spooky action at a distance' — the discussion about reality can support ideas that were previously thought to be fantastical nonsense.[37] Concepts such as multiple universes, holographic universes, virtual realities and inherent mind–matter interaction are considered possible, and worthy of further study.

In December 2007, my husband and I experienced the 'disappearance' of two sets of car keys — an experience that eventually protected us from a significant financial loss, if not actual physical harm. It may be coincidence that we were both rendered blind to the keys that were directly in front of us. However, it is worth noting that the new scientific understanding of psi and the nature of reality offers up other possibilities.

If we were blind to the keys, was it a precognitive reaction? (Did our brains choose to ignore the sight of the car keys, knowing the danger we were about to be placed into?) Alternatively, did the car keys quite literally *disappear* from physical reality for a brief moment? In the new, quantum reality of the 21st century, this possibility, although improbable, is no longer considered impossible.

18

Grill Flame
Fort Meade MD, USA

Mel was almost in the zone. Submerged several metres under the surface of a balmy ocean, he could feel his body entering a state of deep relaxation. His breathing was steady and his mind was clear. With pinpoint focus, Mel gently adjusted his depth. Slowly, deliberately he removed another weight from his diving belt and watched as the sandy ocean floor slipped further away. Above him, the turquoise surface of the water glistened in the sunlight.

Nearly there. Mel released a faint trace of buoyant air and felt his body floating imperceptibly down, down … Suddenly, Mel's mind crackled into life and snippets of images and sensations flooded into his awareness. His preparation was complete. It was time to work…

Mel Riley was not diving in the ocean. He lay inside a darkened room, in a secluded wooden building on the Fort Meade military base in Maryland, USA. The room was sparse, and the single window had been bricked and plastered over. There was a couch, littered with pillows and a blanket, and a single chair. Mel was lying on the couch, entranced in his vision of a turquoise sea.

Beside him, on the chair, another man sat in silent expectation. As the session monitor, his role was to ensure that Mel's work was completed and recorded correctly. He alone had any knowledge of the assignment and, in a sealed envelope, he held clues about the target. More often than not, the simple presence of the envelope would ensure a clear connection with the target but complete misses were sometimes to be expected. Time and space were fickle allies.

Mel and his companion knew the routine well. It was a process they repeated twice, sometimes three times, a day. Mel would make himself comfortable on the couch — shoes off and eyes closed — and begin his mental preparation. In his mind, he would place his daily concerns and distractions into a large, imaginary suitcase. Then, with silent deliberation, he would perform his diving ritual. To Mel, the surface of the water represented full consciousness; the sandy seabed was sleep. He would deliberately float in between, hovering in the shadowy depths of semi-consciousness until he found his 'zone' — a perfect balance of physical relaxation and mental clarity.

Both the suitcase ritual and the diving analogy were relatively new to Mel. He had developed them as part of his current work but mental discipline was something that came naturally. Even as a child, he had often escaped the noisy clatter of his life to find solace in his thoughts.

Mel was born and raised in Racine, a small city nestled between Milwaukee and Chicago on the shores of

Lake Michigan. From a young age, it was apparent to him that he was not suited to urban living — he was always more at home following the relaxed rhythm of nature. By the time he was an adolescent, Mel was often stealing away into the wilderness for days at a time. There, in the grasslands and forests that surrounded Racine, he would take his mind to a quiet place and reclaim his connection with the natural world. At times, he would fish. Other days, he would simply sit and observe the animals. In these early years, Mel developed an intrinsic bond with the land, and with the indigenous people who lived on it.

Like many Native Americans, the Winnebago people of southern Wisconsin had little reason to trust white folk. When Mel first strolled into their presence — a strapping white boy with hypnotic eyes — some in the community were openly dismissive. They questioned his motives and regarded him as a mere 'wannabe'. Few were aware that, as a young child, Mel had been convinced that he was a Native American. It was not curiosity or exploitation that drew him to their communities; it was a deep and powerful magnetism.

Over time, Mel's commitment to the indigenous way of life became apparent. He soon won over the local Winnebago and was welcomed by them. By his mid-teens he had become deeply entrenched in the native community. Day after day, in his spare time, Mel would visit with the elders and immerse himself in Native American culture. Sometimes, he would sit under the watchful eye of Ruth Cloud and the other women — his blonde head bowed over his weaving or beadwork. Other days, he would go hunting with the men.

Sometimes, his wanderings would lead him into more spiritual realms and he would listen quietly to the counsel of a priest or a medicine man. Mel had always felt a deep connection with the unseen. In his childhood had sometimes seen visions and had other mystical experiences. In the humble homes of the Winnebago, he found a place where these experiences were acknowledged and embraced as a natural part of life's journey.

Throughout these early years, many of Mel's visions were fleeting and random, but there was one mystical experience that was both precious and profound — his formal 'vision quest'.

In keeping with the tradition of many Native Americans, Mel's 'vision quest' was regarded as his rite of passage into manhood. When the time came, at the instruction of a local holy man, Mel took himself deep into the wilderness where he fasted, prayed and meditated for four days and nights. In the stillness and serenity of nature, his directive was simple — wait for a mystical vision about his life, his purpose or his true nature. Once that vision had been received, Mel could return to the elder to share his experience.

Mel's boyhood visions, and the ease with which his Winnebago friends accepted them, left a lasting impression on the young man. By 1969, when he was drafted into the US Army at the age of 23, Mel had accepted these insights as a natural part of his experience. Over the next few years, it became apparent that these skills would also help shape his military career.

As soon as he was drafted, Mel was sent for training as a military photo interpreter. He spent the next several years analysing images of enemy interests, gleaning information as part of the military's extensive spying operations. Occasionally, instead of images, Mel was sent to analyse the landscape of enemy countries and he spent many days criss-crossing his way across Eastern Europe in covert spy planes.

It soon became apparent that Mel was good at this job, very good at it, and he quickly gained a reputation as an interpreter with an uncanny sixth sense. Often, he would see things in images that nobody else could decipher. Sometimes he could even describe objects that were physically concealed. Information just seemed to present itself to Mel and nothing, from blurry images to clever camouflage, deterred him. Eventually this extra sensory perception led Mel to another, covert military undertaking — the top secret operation cryptically entitled Grill Flame. It was this project that Mel was now working on.

Lying on the couch in the little wooden building at Fort Meade, Mel began to describe the impressions that were now flashing across his mind. Beside him his companion flicked a switch that triggered a recording device in the next room. Everything Mel said — every image, impression, sensation and insight — would be carefully recorded and collated. The data would then be passed on to whoever had requested the session and the assignment would be complete.

Mel never quite knew how the information would come to him in these sessions. Sometimes it consumed all his senses and he would experience a complete immersion. Other times the connection with the 'target' was more elusive, teasing Mel with fleeting images on the edge of his awareness.

Today the images flowing into Mel's mind were simultaneously familiar and confusing. He had connected with this object before, but this wasn't surprising. In order to collect the best information, each 'target' was normally presented several times over the span of a few weeks. Mel had been given no information about the target, but from what he could tell it was some type of aircraft. The design was foreign to him, completely unlike anything he had seen before. Mel could see the strange bat shaped wings, and the bulb of a cockpit protruding from the top of the plane. He sensed there was something unusual about the aircraft's controls and each time he looked at the lengths of wire running through the plane he saw an odd, bright light — lights in the wires.

Strangest of all, the aircraft seemed to shape-shift in his mind — the details changed every time Mel focused on it. At times, he would describe a strange v-shaped tail, but when he turned his attention to it again the tail would disappear. After several minutes of deep meditative focus, Mel opened his eyes and began to sketch the aircraft. As the images came to life on the paper in front of him, Mel wondered if he had been looking at some kind of toy. "This must be the screwiest thing I've ever seen in my life," he remarked as the session finally drew to a close. "It will never fly," he added.

His companion nodded in silent approval. Mel had produced some great work. Today's target had been a special request from the US Air Force. The plan was to use this target several more times but, for now, the notes and tape recordings from Mel's session would be carefully collected and sent immediately to the Air Force.

Feedback on the accuracy of these session notes was not expected, and rarely received. In this case, however, the team at Grill Flame did receive feedback about Mel's work — almost immediately. It came as an emphatic directive from the Air Force. "Cease and desist," it said. "Terminate the request. Do not attempt to connect with this target again. Forget everything that was seen and discussed in those sessions."

The contents of the yellow envelope — a grainy digital photo — were returned to the Air Force, and the team at Fort Meade never heard from them again.

It would be 10 years before the object that Mel had described was finally revealed. In 1988, after years of intense secrecy, the Pentagon revealed a revolutionary new aircraft — the F-117 Nighthawk. Affectionately dubbed the Stealth Fighter, it had strange bat-like wings and a bulbous cockpit. Sleek and ultramodern, the F-117 included several innovations allowing it to be almost undetectable by radar.

This included the use of fibre optic cabling for the aircraft's controls — Mel's "lights in the wires".

A final mystery was solved for Mel in 1996, when the B-2 stealth bomber was rolled out to the public by the Pentagon. Developed in tandem with the F-117, it shared many of the same features but there was one very obvious difference. The B-2 stealth bomber was designed without the v-shaped tail.

In 1978 Grill Flame was tasked with collecting vital foreign intelligence and they operated for nearly 20 years with high-profile government support, including from Presidents Jimmy Carter and Ronald Reagan. During this time, the team carried out thousands of 'remote viewing' sessions; collecting data about specific 'targets' using only the power of the human mind. Remote viewing sessions were requested by a wide range of military and government departments, such as the US Army, US Air Force, CIA and FBI.

Feedback was not often received on the information provided by remote viewing sessions. However, over time, several stories did emerge of incredible successes, such as the discovery by Joe McMoneagle of the Russian Typhoon class submarine (while it was still under construction), and Mel Riley's uncanny description of the top secret stealth bomber.

Mel Riley was the first full-time operative assigned to Grill Flame in 1978, and he went on to fulfil two separate placements with the team. In 1990, he retired from the program, and from the military, but Riley's work remains an integral part of remote viewing history. He currently enjoys a quiet life in rural Wisconsin where he continues to be actively involved with the Native American community. To this day, stories circulate about the quiet young man who learned the ancient ways of the Native Americans, and later became a legendary remote viewer with the US military 'Psychic Spy' program.

Ancient psi: The modern science of indigenous wisdom

From the perspective of Western science, the evidence for psi and the theories that support its existence are extremely new and confronting. However, as modern advances are made in the fields of psi, consciousness and quantum physics, it is becoming increasingly clear that many of these cutting-edge scientific ideas actually echo the teachings of ancient indigenous peoples.

For instance, the idea of an entangled universe — a concept that is only 50 years old in Western minds — has been the cornerstone of indigenous worldviews for tens of thousands of years. The interconnected nature of the Earth, humans and animals (and in many cases, the spirit world and ancestors) is an integral belief of indigenous people from around the world, including those of Siberia, North America, and Australia.

Curiously, indigenous languages also seem to be highly attuned to the universe at a quantum level. For decades, Western scientists have struggled to find appropriate language to describe the processes and paradoxes of our quantum universe however Native Americans — particularly the Hopi of Arizona — use linguistic structures that seem to describe these concepts perfectly.

It is also worth noting that in all ancient cultures, from Africa to Asia, across the Americas and into Australia and the Pacific, psi experience is regarded as both natural and useful. Mystical visions, psi insight and altered states of consciousness have been an integral part of these cultures for millennia and have often been used to guide, heal and enhance quality of life. Although regarded as a natural phenomenon, it is generally accepted, in ancient cultures, that some people are more skilled at receiving psi information than others, i.e., shamans, medicine doctors and priests of indigenous communities. This, too, is consistent with the findings of modern psi researchers who have noted individual differences in relation to psi abilities.

Over the last few centuries, as Newtonian science took hold in Western society, indigenous cultures came to be regarded as primitive and ill-informed. However, 21st century thinking now gives greater validity to ancient world views, including a greater acceptance of psi. In time, as Western thinking resumes a more holistic approach to science, ancient ideas and understandings may provide clues about the true nature of the universe. Just as Mel Riley

158

was able to draw upon indigenous experiences to succeed in a modern military program, it may be that our future lies in accepting and exploring the teachings of the ancient past.

19

Instinctive and Unfathomable
Phuket, Thailand

Ellie watched the emotions flicker like a shadowy kaleidoscope across Jim's face — frustration, exasperation, anger and a hint of confusion. His grey-blue eyes were flashing cold as ice and he lowered his face close to hers, "You are a freaking psycho. You know that?"

Jim was not an unreasonable man. In fact, he was generally regarded as easy-going, measured and fair. Perhaps these were the very reasons Ellie's insistence had triggered such anger in him. For Jim it didn't matter where they went. It didn't matter when they went. It was Christmas Eve, the next four days were theirs to savour, but Ellie stubbornly persisted and the young Thai woman behind the counter was clearly uncomfortable.

"I am sorry, Ma'am," she repeated, "There are no seats available to the Similan Islands on that day."

Ellie refused to budge. "Can you just check again? I really need to go on that tour. On that day." To Jim, this looked just like another one of Ellie's dramas. His eyes said it all — must you always get your way? His frustration was palpable — Ellie was ruining Christmas Eve and tarnishing their entire Phuket experience.

For a long time, Ellie and Jim had dreamt of travelling to Phuket, to visit the islands of Phi Phi. In 1995, and again in 2000, the couple had planned a trip to the popular holiday destination but each time, for one reason or another (and despite making it to Bangkok) their plans for Phuket had never come to fruition. Finally, nine years after their first intended visit, Jim and Ellie landed in the lush solitude of Phuket airport. Ahead of them were five days of tropical bliss — recreation, fun and, of course, snorkelling in the pristine waters off Phi Phi.

Within minutes of their arrival, as they rode towards their hotel in the airport shuttle van, Ellie was considering a change of plan. The vehicle was crammed with brochures of local attractions, tours and cultural highlights — stately Buddhist temples, pulsing Patong nightclubs, luxurious sandy beaches. Dozens of brightly illustrated leaflets, showing tanned and energetic tourists and beaming local children, hung precariously from the two front seats. However, for Ellie, one brochure stood out like a beacon from the rest — Boat Tours to the Similan Islands.

Two years earlier the unexpected death of Jim's brother Simon had sent ripples of devastation through the whole family. Both Jim and Ellie loved Simon deeply and, holding the brochure for Similan Island, Ellie felt time and distance disappear. It was nearly two years since his death yet, with this simple reminder in her hands, Ellie felt a deep and profound connection to Simon.

"Let's go here instead of Phi Phi," she had said to Jim. "It reminds me of Simon and it looks like a nice place to go snorkelling." Jim offered a brief, noncommittal response and by the time they had arrived at their hotel the brochure had been discarded and forgotten.

The Kamala Bay Resort boasted the kind of picture-perfect location that the tropics deliver with breathtaking frequency. Nestled on a craggy, thickly-forested hillside, the resort overlooked an expanse of golden sand and azure waters. Closest to the beach, the breezy lobby and restaurant were located next to a sparkling swimming pool. Further up the steep slope lay the scattered hotel villas, their tiled roofs sitting like terracotta mushrooms above the treetops.

It was exquisite; it was paradise. It was exactly what Ellie had imagined her Phuket experience would be — except for one small detail. The room they had been assigned was at the very top of the resort. It had a magnificent view but required an arduous climb.

The trek up to their room made Ellie cranky. "Seriously, do you think they could have placed us closer to the pool?" she complained as they hiked the steep trail. "We come here for an enjoyable holiday and they put us at the very top of a bloody hill." Ellie's sense of injustice had been ignited. She was the first to admit that she had a strong will, and she was not afraid to exert it if she felt cheated or taken advantage of in any way. Jim had simply laughed off her mood. They were finally in Phuket and he was content.

The following morning, Ellie and Jim headed to the beach in search of action and adventure. They were not inclined to spend their holidays sunbathing or lying around in dreamy self-reflection. They had decided to hire a jet-ski and spent the entire morning laughing, splashing and playing on the sapphire waters of Kamala Bay. As they stumbled back ashore, glowing with amusement and giddy as children, they decided they simply had to repeat the jet-ski experience later in the week.

"How about on the 26th?" Jim suggested. "No," Ellie replied promptly. "We'll go on our diving trip that day." Ellie liked to be organised and she enjoyed her holidays most when they were structured and well planned. Tomorrow, Christmas Day, would be quiet and intimate. Boxing Day, seemed to Ellie the most appropriate time to head offshore.

By dusk, Ellie's itinerary had cemented itself in her mind. She was sure she wanted to snorkel on Boxing Day. Jet-skiing could wait until the following day and tonight, Christmas Eve, they would explore Patong Beach.

By the time they arrived in their tuk-tuk, the Patong Night Market was in full swing. The tightly packed shops and stalls stretched right down the beach road, offering a wide assortment of edible delights, garments, fabrics and brand-name goods of questionable origin. As with many Asian markets, it was loosely organised mayhem — a vibrant veneer of 'business' that threatened to dissolve into pure chaos at any moment. The lanes were crowded and the prices inflated but the colours, sounds and smells of the market enticed tourists from all over Phuket to come, and to spend.

It was here, in the market, that Ellie and Jim spied the booking office for diving and boat tours. The discussion about where and when to travel had begun even before they entered the office. "It doesn't matter if it's Phi Phi or Similan," Jim offered. "It's just snorkelling. Once we're in the water it'll all look the same." But Ellie held firm. She needed to go to Similan — it was as if she had to go.

"I am sorry, Ma'am," the young woman at the counter said. "There are no seats available to the Similan Islands on that day." Ellie refused to take no for an answer. Jim was becoming increasingly irate and still Ellie persisted — obstinate and irrational. "No, it has to be that tour," she reiterated, and an awkward confrontation began.

Ellie watched the shadows in Jim's eyes as his mood swung from exasperation, to rage, to indignation. As the couple argued, the young Thai woman was visibly uncomfortable. "We do have seats to Phi Phi that day," she offered hopefully.

"Yes," replied Jim. "We always said Phi Phi."

"It is a much closer destination, Ma'am," the young woman continued. "The travelling time is much shorter on that tour."

At any other time, Ellie may have complained and begrudgingly booked an alternative — but not today. Today Ellie's need was instinctive — unfathomable. She wasn't trying to be disruptive — she understood the obvious limitations the young woman was working within.

Rationally, she could see that there were other days and other locations available but, somehow, she knew it was really, really important that they book their diving tour to the Similan Islands on 26 December. Ellie did not stop to analyse her motivation — all that mattered was finding a way to do what she felt, overwhelmingly, she had to do.

"It absolutely matters that we get on that tour," she stated.

In resignation, the young woman picked up the phone and started dialling. Jim was muttering obscenities under his breath. Within minutes, there was good news. "There are two places available for Similan on 26 December."

Jim's threw his hands in the air in utter exasperation. Ellie knew that, right now, he didn't want to go anywhere with her. "Thank you," Ellie sighed. "We'll take them."

Many times in the past, Ellie had won a battle of wills and asserted her needs. She was familiar with getting her own way. She knew the thrill of victory, the warm glow of contentment. But now, in this moment, she felt none of those familiar feelings of triumph. All she felt was a palpable relief — an emotional alignment — as if all was now right in the world.

As they left the office, Ellie offered an apology, "I'm sorry Jim. I just really, really need to go that day," she said. But her words fell on deaf ears. Jim was fed up, dismissive — not interested in Ellie's apology. Ellie said nothing more. Their arguments never festered and she knew Jim would soon be smiling at her again.

******

Boxing Day 2004 promised to be hot and humid in Phuket and even as the sun rose over the forested hillsides, bulky clouds were gathering overhead. It was an early start for Ellie and Jim, making their way down the steep hillside from their hotel room in the brightening dawn to meet their 7am tour van. Once collected, the couple bumped along in the back of the vehicle for over an hour as they headed north, off Phuket Island and up the coast of mainland Thailand. By now, any trace of the dispute in the booking office had melted away and Ellie and Jim were eager and excited to reach the Similan Islands.

At Tap Lamu pier, Ellie and Jim joined the crowds of holiday makers that had gathered from destinations across south-west Thailand. Among them, bustling tour operators with clipboards were gently shooing passengers into groups, checking names and shepherding people toward their vessels.

Their boat to the Similan Islands was modern, sleek and comfortable and, with its two powerful engines, built for speed. Ellie and Jim clambered on board with around 20 other passengers, but they didn't depart for at least another hour.

Somehow in the process of boarding, one passenger had gone missing, so the sun was already creeping above the eastern hilltops when the crew eventually powered up the engines and they set off. It was after 9:15am — they were the last boat to leave.

The 50km trip to Similan usually took about an hour. Once underway, Ellie settled herself down where she could feel the wind in her hair and view the depths of the crystal-clear water. The sky overhead was agate blue, the scenery was spectacular and Ellie was entranced and content.

The swell came about 15 minutes into the journey, soon after they rounded the spit that lies protectively in front of Tap Lamu harbour. It was nothing more than a rise on the ocean; an almost imperceptible bump on the undulating surface, but something about it captured Ellie's momentary attention. Maybe it was the way the powerful boat landed with a reverberating 'boom'; perhaps it was the sudden complaint of nausea from a fellow passenger.

Looking over the side of the boat, Ellie was taken with the incredible colour of the water. It was dark, and strange black orbs swirled and danced under the surface. From the depths, a mass of bubbles began to rise and tiny, shimmering vibrations danced on the tops of the waves. *I wonder if there's a whale shark down there*, Ellie thought to herself. She breathed in the hot, salty air and relaxed back into the rhythm of the throbbing engines.

The sea looked weird, but it also looked beautiful, clear and inviting. Ellie could not wait to reach the Similan Islands so that she could jump into its cool embrace.

It took just over an hour for the tour boat to reach the waters off Similan. It was only then that confusion and disbelief began to unravel around Ellie and the other travellers. Here, the water was calm but murky brown and dead crabs and shellfish floated on the surface. Tour boats from a variety of companies and ports had all gathered near the islands and crew members were shouting animatedly to other boats and anxiously talking into their radios.

It took some time for the jumble of Thai conversation to be clarified and translated for the passengers on board. There has been a cyclone. No, not a cyclone. A big wave. A tsunami. Not long after that bloodied and beaten tourists began to be hoisted on board. These were the early morning divers and swimmers — those who had arrived early or had stayed overnight on the islands. Ellie stared in amazement at the broken bodies, dragged across razor-sharp coral as the tsunami had sucked them out to sea and then cruelly hurled them back onto the rocky islands.

But it was the view that eventually greeted Ellie back on the mainland shore that left her most shocked. Travelling slowly, unsure of where they could dock, the crew guided the boat back into Tap Lamu harbour. Here, the water was thick with mud, and trees and other flotsam littered its surface. The pier was gone; where there was once a huddle of buildings there now lay a jumble of muddy debris. On the hillside nearby, a Navy ship was wedged precariously between the trees. Everything on shore, everything that had stood there a few hours earlier, was gone. All that remained, as if in eerie defiance, was a lone vegetable stand stocked full of fresh produce.

Ellie couldn't comprehend the devastation before her eyes. They had felt nothing on the boat — not even a hint of the destructive power that had slammed the shore.

Once off the vessel Ellie and Jim were told to run, and they did. For the next 24 hours, Ellie and Jim clung to each other, finding shelter in an old monastery and an empty home. When they finally got back to their resort, exhausted and hungry, they discovered the hotel in ruins. The road was badly damaged, the lobby and pool were completely gone and the nearby village obliterated. But one thing remained. High on the hill, that uncomfortable climb above the lobby, Ellie and Jim's room sat untouched and inviting.

To this day, Ellie attributes their survival in Phuket to a protective presence — an unknown force that kept her and Jim safe in a time of terrible tragedy. If they had chosen any other activity that day — jet-skiing in Kamala Bay, sightseeing in Patong or snorkelling near Phi Phi — it is almost certain that they would have been caught in the full brunt of the tsunami.

Ellie's curious impulse and her stubborn insistence that she follow her instinct meant that they sailed over history's most destructive tsunami and felt nothing more than a memorable 'bump'.

Ellie and Jim currently live in South East Asia with their young children. They returned to visit Phuket in 2014.

Note: Names in the above story have been changed to protect the subjects' privacy

Animal instinct: Primal psi

The invention of agriculture around 10,000 years ago heralded the beginning of human civilisation and forever changed our perception of nature and the role we play within it. Today, most modern lives are so far removed from natural processes and habits that we have detached ourselves from our identity as part of the animal kingdom. But, no matter how much we have developed, we remain animals.

We share incredible biological, chemical and sociological similarities with our animal cousins and we are still influenced by natural (sometimes primitive) instincts and reactions. The humble hiccup, for instance, is believed to stem from the need for gill ventilation — an instinct present in one of our ancient marine ancestors around 370 million years ago.[38] The ability to laugh (a strange sociological behaviour) arose in our ancestors hundreds of thousands of years ago and is also present in chimpanzees, bonobos, orangutan and possibly even rats.[39]

One of the most intriguing traits that many non-human animals display is the apparent familiarity with, and practical use of, psi information. This animal sixth sense has been observed for thousands of years and has been the subject of intense research. In 1919, naturalist William Long published what is widely regarded as the most complete field research ever produced on the subject of silent animal communication. His extended observations on wolves, caribou, foxes and other wild animals led Long to conclude that a wide array of animals display evidence of telepathic communication and, sometimes, uncanny precognition.[40]

Long's work has inspired many modern researchers including the biologist Rupert Sheldrake who has documented incredible evidence of pets that appear to know when their human companions are on their way home, even when this return is spontaneous or unexpected.[41]

Interestingly, history also provides numerous accounts of animals reacting to natural disasters and other calamities before they occur. One of the most cited examples is the earthquake and tsunami that destroyed Melice in Greece in 373 B.C. According to contemporary writers, snakes, rats and other small animals were seen fleeing the city in the five days leading up to the disaster. During World War II, dozens of pet animals on both sides of the English Channel (in Britain and Germany) reportedly exhibited an ability to regularly predict incoming bombs — even, in some cases, when those bombs were supersonic V2 rockets. In the days before the 1997 earthquake in Assisi, Italy there were many reports of animals in the local area acting strangely. In one case, a local village was overrun with large rats a week before the quake hit.

The tragic tsunami of Boxing Day 2004 offers other incredible examples of this animal instinct for self-preservation. All across South East Asia, stories have emerged of animals reacting in advance to the earthquake and tsunami. Elephants in Thailand, Sri Lanka and Indonesia were observed running up the hillsides prior to the disaster, some of them trumpeting as they fled. In Bang Koey, Thailand a villager noticed a herd of buffalo who had been grazing by the beach suddenly lift their heads, stare out to sea and then stampede up the hill to higher ground. In Yala National Park, in coastal Sri Lanka, park rangers were surprised to discover that only two water buffalo had perished in the tsunami. All the wildlife in the park, including elephants, leopards, bears and hundreds of species of wading bird, had moved far from the shoreline before the wave struck.

There are many theories as to what animals are reacting to in these situations. Some say they are attuned to tiny seismic vibrations or to the release of gases from the earth prior to an earthquake. However, seismology does not pick up any such vibrations, and the animals who fled the 2004 tsunami were not all in the earthquake zone, but along the coasts that were soon to be flooded. Also, oncoming disasters are often too far away to be heard — even by the keenest ears.

It is, therefore, reasonable to consider that, at times, animals react to some form of psi information when danger is approaching — a theory that sits well with those who work closely with animals. Roger Hoppes, the San Francisco Zoo's vice president of operations said in a 2011 interview, "I'm never surprised anymore about the sensitivities of animals being able to perceive things or react to things or sense things that are beyond my individual skills. I wouldn't put <precognitive ability> past them."[42]

Taking into account our inescapable kinship with the animal kingdom, it is logical to assume that humans too are attuned to psi information through some form of animal instinct — particularly if we, or our closest companions, are in danger. Given our modern detachment from natural habits, it is likely that these instincts are now less developed and underutilised but, as in Ellie's case, they may still be acute enough to 'click in' in times of great peril.

In Phuket in 2004, something deep and primal inside Ellie overrode any logical thought. She did not feel a specific sense of impending danger. She did not have a premonition or precognition. She reacted to a profound, instinctive need. She simply followed an instinct that, with hindsight, she realised had taken her out of danger.

In this respect, Ellie's experience closely resembles the actions of animals (wild and domesticated) that instinctively withdraw themselves from impending danger, without the ability to understand or rationalise their behaviour.

There are obvious, practical advantages to acknowledging and harnessing the ability of animals to predict natural disasters; so much so that some nations have adopted animal observation as part of their formal earthquake monitoring methods.

20

An Exceptional Man

Berkeley CA, USA

To the casual observer, there was nothing special about Pat Price — a stocky middle-aged man, slightly dishevelled, with an even temper and a jovial and forthright disposition. A Scientologist and semi-retired businessman, Pat made a living growing Christmas trees and managing a building contractor firm out of his base in Lake Tahoe, California. Pat Price was respectable, and respected, but not particularly remarkable for most people, even though he'd been the mayor of Burbank and its Police Commissioner.

However, for many, Pat Price was exceptional. When described by the CIA, he was labelled extraordinary and unbelievable; a NASA physicist regarded him as unprecedented and a US Congressional Committee heard him described as miraculous.

While Pat Price was a regular American guy who loved to fish and play poker he was also the most incredible psychic the US government had ever seen.

That is why, on Tuesday, 5 February 1974, the Berkeley Police Department came to him for help. The daughter of one of the most powerful men in California had disappeared and her fate was a complete mystery.

The call had come in to the Stanford Research Institute (SRI) in the afternoon. The SRI was where Pat conducted most of his official psychic work. By now, the news outlets were feverish with the story of 19-year-old Patty Hearst, daughter of publishing magnate, Randolph Hearst who'd been brutally kidnapped from her Berkeley apartment the previous night. The pressure on the police to crack this case — and to crack it quickly — was immense, but leads were few and far between. The perpetrators were still completely unknown. There had been no contact; no demands.

Pat was no stranger to psychic police work. As the Burbank Police Commissioner, he had honed his skills in the radio control room, listening in to developing situations and offering his intuitive impressions of where the offenders might be found. Over time, he began to receive psychic insights on a daily basis but it was only more recently, through his work at SRI, that Pat had become involved in governmental matters and international espionage.

When the request came in, Pat was happy to oblige and within hours he was standing in Apartment 4, 2603 Benvenue Street, Berkeley — Patty Hearst's empty home. An impression came to him immediately. "This isn't about money," he advised to the shock of everyone present. Randolph Hearst's fortune was an obvious target for criminals and it was expected that a ransom demand would arrive soon. But Pat was adamant. "This is political. The kidnapping is designed as a terrorist act. They want publicity, sympathy," he concluded.

At the police station, Pat continued his intuitive investigation. Standing at a large oak table in the station house, he slowly browsed the station's mug shot book. Career criminals, wayward juveniles, questionable characters — thousands of unidentified, scowling faces stared back at Pat as he flipped through the loose-leaf folder. Suddenly his finger stabbed. "There. Him. That's the ringleader," he announced. Detectives quickly checked and identified the man under Pat's finger as Donald DeFreeze; a repeat violent offender with schizophrenic tendencies and a love for homemade explosives.

Pat continued to turn the pages and his finger stabbed twice more. "Him. And him," Pat remarked.

"This one keeps giving me the name Lobo," he explained. The detectives frowned. Lobo; the Spanish word for wolf. "It feels like he is like me; a kindred spirit. He is shamanic and has incredible mind control." The others stood in amazement as Pat continued. "He had a tooth extracted at the dentist recently and he did it without anaesthesia. Instead, he used self-hypnosis."

The detective in charge spoke up. "Where are they now?" he enquired. Pat's answer was immediate and confident. He raised his arm and pointed north. "They went that way," he said. "I see a white station wagon near a restaurant. It's across from the highway from two large gas storage tanks, near an overpass."

The description was concise and accurate. "I know where that is!" exclaimed one of the detectives. "It's on the way to my home, in Vallejo." A police car was dispatched immediately and within 10 minutes, the call came in. The car had been found, exactly as Pat had described, and with bullet shells, matching those in Hearst's apartment, scattered on the vehicle's floor.

It was only 48 hours before Pat's extraordinary accuracy was highlighted again. After three days of sinister silence, the culprits contacted a local radio station and outlined their demands. The group called themselves the *Symbionese Liberation Army* (SLA); a posse of left-wing radicals, anarchists and extremists who had no interest in conventional cash ransoms.

Instead, their intent was to wage guerrilla warfare against what they termed the "capitalist state". They demanded that the Hearst family provide foodstuffs to every underprivileged person in the San Francisco Bay area in order to secure Patty's release.

Detectives worked quickly to research more about the group, and what they discovered astounded them. The three men Pat had targeted in the Berkeley police station were all members of the SLA. Donald "Cinque Mtume" DeFreeze was the gang leader; another man in the trio was a Berkeley dropout called William Wolfe; or as he was sometimes known "Willy the Wolf". Further digging about Wolfe revealed one extraordinary fact. Police confirmed that he had recently had a tooth removed at the dentists and had done so without any anaesthesia.

For several weeks, Pat Price continued to work on the Hearst case; to find where she had been hidden and help initiate a rescue. Although he was able to visualise Patty locked in a cupboard somewhere (a fact that later emerged as accurate), he was unable to pinpoint the location of the dwelling or psychically read any of the street signs in her vicinity.

The Hearst family immediately spent two million dollars on feeding the underprivileged in the Bay Area, however the SLA determined that a further six million dollars should be spent. The kidnapping case reached an impasse. Then, on 15 April 1974, Patty was spotted participating in an armed robbery of a San Francisco bank. It appeared that she was no longer a captive of the SLA, but rather an active supporter of their cause.

Pat continued his work with SRI, various government agencies and corporate interests until his death in a Las Vegas hotel in July 1975. Deemed to be a simple heart attack, rumours still abound that his death was assisted by the secret workings of an unknown agency. Even in his death, Pat Price managed to overcome the mundane and become something extraordinary.

Applied Psi: Predicting the future of psi

In 2008, British psychologist and prominent sceptic, Richard Wiseman, admitted to the *Daily Mail* that, "by the standards of any other area of science remote viewing is proven". He later went on to clarify that he meant *all psi phenomena,* not just remote viewing, had met the standards of accepted scientific rigour.

The empirical evidence in favour of the existence of psi is regarded, by many, as overwhelming. Therefore, psi researchers are steadily turning their attention away from proof of psi, toward a more practical understanding of how these phenomena can be harnessed and utilised in everyday life. As we look to the future, it may be reasonable to assume that psi will be most effective in those areas where it has already been employed. Law enforcement is one such area.

Over the years, anecdotes have emerged of police departments calling on psi professionals to help solve tough cases. The story of Pat Price and the Patty Hearst kidnapping case is one such occasion. According to author Arthur Lyons and sociologist Marcello Truzzi, around 10% of law enforcement officials have accepted psi input as part their investigations, although most cases are not publicised.[43] In 2015, the occasional accuracy of psi input was officially recognised by the UK Police College, when their revised guidelines included the directive that psi information offered in missing person investigations should not be disregarded.

Anecdotes have also emerged of psi influence in courtroom jury selections, the training of fire fighters and rescue teams, and, in commercial application, the discovery of precious deposits such as oil and archaeological sites. Pat Price, in fact, was employed at one stage to discover valuable coal seams for a company in the hills of West Virginia, USA.

Psi in the realm of medicine, is another intriguing area — particularly in the area of early diagnosis of disease. The topic of psi diagnostics has been raised at official medical gatherings, including conferences for the Society for Medical Decision Making and the National Institutes of Health, Office of Alternative Medicine. In the public domain, anecdotal evidence has emerged of dogs being able to intuitively predict both the presence of cancer and epileptic seizures. At this point in time, however, scientific exploration of medically-based psi is in its infancy.

Perhaps unsurprisingly, the future of psi as a practical tool may be most closely tied to its feasibility in two areas — military endeavours and commerce.

The use of a sixth sense in battle dates back as far as 500BC, when the Chinese general, Sun Tzu, in the original *Art of War*, describes the importance of enhancing military tactics and manoeuvres with the use of *ch'i*, or life force.

More recently, in World War II, psi abilities are reputed to have aided the Allied Forces in their defeat of Hitler's Nazis. In one example, official documents declassified in 1970 reveal that this was the case for British RAF commander, Lord Hugh Dowding (often dubbed 'the man who won the Battle of Britain'). Dowding was often assisted by his wife, Clarice who, it seems, was a 'sensitive' who would use her remote viewing skills to provide feedback on the location of undetected enemy airbases.

As discussed in Chapter 18, several countries have historically engaged the skills of psi spies for military and government agencies. We don't know whether this covert practice continues today. However, the use of psi does pose obvious advantages as a safe, effective (and cost effective) form of intelligence gathering.

In the commercial marketplace, the idea of being the first to tap into mind–matter interactions such as telekinesis (explained in Chapter 17) has proven irresistible for some. Most notably, technology giant Sony, with the blessing of company co-founder, Masara Ibuka, conducted a seven-year study into psi. Based in a secret arm of the company named the Institute of Wisdom, Sony's research team produced research results that suggested the existence of psi. Some results were, perhaps, a bit too incredible and in 1998, soon after the death of Ibuka, the program was discontinued.

More covert experiments have been undertaken by other technology companies; leading psi researcher, Dean Radin, has personally overseen research at Bell

Laboratories and Contel Technology Center where he explored the concept of psi interaction with electronic circuitry.[44]

The scientific discoveries of the past century have forever changed our understanding of the material universe and the way we interact with it. As we move further into an era of quantum reality, it is inevitable that we will encounter new horizons and new possibilities.

At this astonishing turning point in science, we have two choices: we can repeat the patterns of the past and resist new ideas, or we can choose to leap forward from what may have been the abyss of ignorance and trust that human experience and capability offers clues to all we need to know.

Perhaps for those brave enough to explore those facets of the mind, the possibilities are, indeed, infinite.

Tips and Tools

It is understood by psi researchers that the ability to receive and interpret psi information is ubiquitous in the human population.

Below are some tips and tools that I have found effective in my personal coaching sessions. These tips are based on scientific research and personal experience and, I believe, are helpful for anyone striving to develop their psi abilities.

Develop your 'right-brain' processes
A simple way to strengthen your natural psi connection is to improve your right-brain functioning.

- Become more creative; take time to express yourself through art or creative writing
- Give your mind a rest; take time to enjoy stillness or relaxing music
- Practise getting into an intuitive flow; use automatic writing or drawing to express yourself
- Ask questions, and allow the images or words to flow, without controlling or labelling the information.

Practice self-awareness
Psi information often causes subtle, yet noticeable, changes in your body, mind and emotions. Therefore, self-

awareness is a key to recognising psi information when it is received.

Take some time to learn your 'default setting'; your natural state of being. During a time of rest, pay attention to the following aspects.

- What is your body's natural level of relaxation? When at rest, do you feel comfortable and at ease, or are there natural areas of tension? Do you feel tranquil and calm, or are you energised and poised for action?
- How is your body responding physiologically? Does your skin feel cold; warm; hot? Are there any tingling or numb areas on your body? Does your gut feel calm and quiet, or is it displaying signs of gurgling, churning or tension?
- What is your natural emotional state? Turn your attention to your underlying emotions. Are you, at a fundamental level, happy and content; anxious and fearful; upset and aggrieved?
- And, finally, recognise the natural state of your mind. Is it clear and quiet; zen-like? Is it frantic with thoughts and/or creative inspiration? Does it flow with steady and effortless mental activity? Do your thoughts match your natural emotional state, or are these two aspects independent of each other?

It is important not to judge any aspect of yourself as you conduct this exercise; there is no right, nor wrong. Simply recognise and accept these elements *exactly as they present themselves*. You can then use them as your natural point of reference when recognising psi information.

Once you have determined your default setting, you are better equipped to notice the subtle changes that occur if, and when, you are receiving psi information. This information can manifest itself as unusual or unexpected changes in your mind, body or emotional state; a slight change in mood, increased or decreased energy levels, physiological changes or repetitive, vivid or unusual thought patterns.

Work with your natural psi strengths

Psi information is perhaps most accurately described as a form of 'data'; it arrives in your unconscious as pure knowledge, information, or awareness. In order for it to be recognised and understood, the conscious brain then converts that data into a vision, audible sound, thought or sensation.

In my experience, an individual's psi connection will be stronger in one or two areas: clairvoyance, clairaudience, clairsentience or claircognizance.

Your mental aptitudes and preferences can offer a key to your (probable) psi strengths. For instance, if you tend to learn and process information visually, have a photographic memory and/or have strong visualisation skills, it is likely that psi information will be interpreted by your brain as clairvoyance. If you are highly empathic, emotionally sensitive and/or often have physical reactions to people and events (such as prickly skin or butterflies in the stomach) you are likely to receive psi knowledge in clairsentient form. Individuals with a memory for tunes, poetry and lyrics, and those who learn best through aural stimulation are likely to interpret psi information as clairaudience.

Learning to recognise how your conscious mind usually delivers psi information to you is an important step in strengthening your psi connection.

Relax and let go

Psi ability appears to be similar to creative inspiration; it is an intangible 'flow' of information that sits outside rationale and logic. Therefore, it may be more difficult to recognise or consciously interpret psi information if you:

- rely heavily on logic and rational thinking
- have strong left-brain tendencies
- are over-eager to receive psi information, or try to force or control the process.

For the most profound and accurate psi information, it is important to quieten the logical mind and simply allow the information to filter into your awareness without the need to analyse, explain or label what you are experiencing.

Notes

Introduction
1. According to cosmologists, only 4.6% of the universe — matter and energy — can be measured by human technology. The vast majority of the universe (95.4%) is Dark Matter and Dark Energy, which is completely invisible and unfathomable to us. Although we don't know what these forces are, it is possible that they affect us in every single moment.

Prologue
2. As described in *The Hitchhiker's Guide to the Universe*, created by Douglas Adams.
3. Poll: 71% of respondents admitted to having some form of paranormal experience. (www.about.com Paranormal Poll)

A Strange and Intense Dream
4. Based on cross-cultural surveys: Stevenson & Prasad, 1968 and Rhine, 1964

A Silent Force
5. *The Presence of the Past: Morphic Resonance and the Habits of Nature*, R. Sheldrake, 1988

Quiet Epiphany
6. The first image of this phenomena was released in 2015 by a research team at École Polytechnique Fédérale de Lausanne
7. 'Entangling macroscopic diamonds at room temperature', (2011) Science 334 (6060): 1253–1256. Lee, Sprague et al.

The Clear and Insistent Thought
8. *The daemon of Socrates: a paper read before the Royal Institution*, Jan. 26, 1872 (1872)

Buckle In Tight
9. As explained in *The Way of the Explorer*, Edgar Mitchell.

10   As explained in *Life before Life*, Jim B. Tucker.

11.   Patricia Kuhl: *The linguistic genius of babies* (Presentation at TEDxRainier, Oct 2010)

12.   This includes research on cognitive dissonance (Festinger), memory distortion (Schacter) and illusory perception (Lotto).

To Be an Artist

13.   For example, "And the angel of the Lord appeared unto him in a flame of fire out of the midst of a bush: and he looked, and, behold, the bush burned with fire, and the bush was not consumed." Exodus 3:2 *King James Bible (1611)*; "It is no less than inspiration sent down to him: He was taught by one Mighty in Power, Endued with Wisdom: for he appeared (in stately form); While he was in the highest part of the horizon: Then he approached and came closer, And was at a distance of but two bow-lengths or even nearer;"*[Quran 53:4–9]*

The Sudden Awakening

14.   Name changed to protect subject's privacy

15.   For example, "Jesus perceived their thoughts" Luke 5:22; "For the Lord searcheth all hearts, and understandeth all the imaginations of the thoughts" 1 Corinthians 28:9, *King James Bible (1611)*

16.   As outlined in 'The Mysteries of Twins', *The Washington Post*, 11 January 1998

17.   Results summarised in *The Conscious Universe*, Dr Dean Radin.

18.   As with dream telepathy and the Ganzfeld technique.

A Heavy Void

19.   *Evidence of correlated functional MRI signals between distant human brains*, Standish et al, 2004

20.   *Gut feelings, intuition and emotions: An exploratory study*, Radin & Schiltz, 2005

Connie's Hunch

21.   Noted by Russell Targ et al, in numerous remote-viewing experiments.

The Chosen One

22. 'Six Tales of Courage: Ihsan Khan — A Dollar and a Desi Dream', Time, 19 December 2005

23. *Can dreams intuit winning lottery numbers?*, Randall Fitzgerald, examiner.com, 2009

Who is Dead in the White House?

24. Excerpts from *The Mother's Vision,* by Asia Booth, written 2 June 1854 (published in *John Wilkes Booth: A Sister's Memoir,* by Asia Booth Clarke, 1938)

25. Conversation between Abraham Lincoln, Mary Lincoln and Ward Hill Lamon, as quoted in *Recollections of Abraham Lincoln 1847–1865*, by Ward Hill Lamon

26. Article in *The New York Times,* Friday, 14 April 1865

27. As told in *The Personal Memoirs of Julia Dent Grant (Mrs Ulysses S. Grant)*, edited by John Y. Simon

28. *Future Telling: A meta-analysis of forced-choice precognition experiments*, 1935-1987, Honorton and Ferrari, Journal of Parapsychology, 53

29. *Feeling the Future: Experimental Evidence for Anomalous Retroactive Influences on Cognition and Affect*, Daryl J. Bem, 2011, Journal of Personality and Social Psychology, 100

30. As described in *The Conscious Universe: The Scientific Truth of Psychic Phenomena*, Dean Radin

I Saw Her Too

31. From *Memoirs of a Mountain Guide,* Lou Whittaker and Andrea Gabbard

32. *Psi vs. survival: A qualitative investigation of mediums' phenomenology comparing psychic readings and ostensible communication with the deceased,* Rock, Beischel & Cott, 2009

Jesse Couldn't Resist

33. *Viewing the Future: A Pilot Study with an Error-Detecting Protocol,* (Targ, Katra, Brown & Wiegand), 1995

34. 'Did Psychic Powers Give Firm a Killing In the Silver Market? And Did Greed Ruin It All?', Erik Larson, Wall Street Journal. (Eastern edition). New York, N.Y.: Oct 22, 1984. pg. 1

35. *Stock Market Prediction Using Associative Remote Viewing by Inexperienced Remote Viewers*, (Smith, Laham & Moddel), 2013

Angry Mist and Thunderous Noise

36. Bernard d'Espagnat, *Scientific American 1979*
37. Frequently attributed to Albert Einstein, as his description for quantum entanglement.

Instinctive and Unfathomable

38. 'A phylogenetic hypothesis for the origin of hiccough', BioEssays 25/2, C. Straus, K. Vasilakos (2003)
39. 'Animals and Sociology', Leslie Irvine, Sociology Compass 2/6 (2008)
40. *How Animals Talk: And Other Pleasant Studies of Birds and Beasts*, William Long (1919)
41. *Dogs That Know When Their Owners are Coming Home*, Rupert Sheldrake (2011)
42. http://www.sfgate.com/science/article/Do-zoo-animals-forecast-quakes-other-disasters-2310058.php

An Exceptional Man

43. *The Blue Sense: Psychic Detectives and Crime*, Arthur Lyon and Marcello Truzzi
44. As outlined in *The Noetic Universe*, Dean Radin

Selected References

Booth Clarke, A and Alford, T (ed) (1996) *John Wilkes Booth: A Sister's Memoir*, Jackson, MS: University Press of Mississippi

Churchill, WS (1900) *London to Ladysmith via Pretoria*, London: Longmans, Green and Company

Churchill, WS (1996) *My Early Life 1874–1904*, New York: Scribner; 5.7.1996 edition

Coffey, M. (2008) *Explorers of the Infinite*, New York: Penguin

Hilton, CN (1987) *Be My Guest*, New York: Prentice Hall Press

Irvine, L (2008) 'Animals and Sociology', Sociology Compass, 2/6, 1954–1971

Lamon, WH and Teillard (Lamon), D (ed) (1911) *Recollections of Abraham Lincoln 1847–1865*, Chicago: AC McClurg and Company

Lefevre, E (1923) *Reminiscences of a Stock Operator*, New York: John Wiley and Sons

Long, WJ (1919) *How Animals Talk: And Other Pleasant Studies of Birds and Beasts*, New York: Harper and Brothers

McEneaney, B (2010) *Messages*, New York: William Morrow

Manning, HE (2013) *The Daemon of Socrates: A Paper, 1872.* London: Forgotten Books. Reprint

Martinez, SB (2009) *The Psychic Life of Abraham Lincoln*, Franklin Lakes, NJ: New Page Books

Melton, JG (ed) (1996) *Encyclopaedia of Occultism and Parapsychology*, Detroit: Gale Group; 4th edition

Mitchell, ED (2008) *The Way of the Explorer*, Franklin Lakes, NJ: New Page Books

O'Murchu, D (2012) *In the Beginning Was the Spirit*, Maryknoll, NY: Orbis

Parry, GA (Dec 2005–Feb 2006) 'Native Wisdom in a Quantum World', Shift: At the Frontiers of Consciousness, 9, 29–33

Powell, DH (Mar-May 2009) 'Twin Telepathy and the Illusion of Separation', Shift: At the Frontiers of Consciousness, 22, 20

Radin, D (1997) *The Conscious Universe*, New York: HarperCollins

Radin, D (2006) *Entangled Minds*, New York: Pocket Books

Radin, D (2013) *Supernormal*, New York: Deepak Chopra Books

Schnabel, J (1997) *Remote Viewers*, New York: Dell Publishing

Sheldrake, R (2011) *Dogs That Know When Their Owners are Coming Home*, New York: Three Rivers Press

Sheldrake, R (2012) *Science Set Free*, New York: Deepak Chopra Books

Shuster, M. (1987) *Power, Pathology, Paradox: The Dynamics of Evil and Good*, Grand Rapids, MI: Zondervan

Simon, JY (ed) (1975) *The Personal Memoirs of Julia Dent Grant (Mrs Ulysses S. Grant)*, New York: Southern Illinois University Press. Reprint.

Targ, R (2012) *The Reality of ESP*, Wheaton, IL: Quest Books

Tucker, J. (2005) *Life Before Life*, New York: St Martin's Griffin

Walsh, R (2007) *The World of Shamanism: New Views of an Ancient Tradition*, Woodbury, MN: Llewellyn

Whitaker, L. and Gabbard, A. (1994) *Memoirs of a Mountain Guide*, Seattle: The Mountaineers

Wilson, N (ed) (2006) *Encyclopedia of Ancient Greece*, New York: Routledge

About the Author

Kim Forrester is a mother, nature lover, global traveller, holistic well-being advocate and kindness enthusiast. As an award-winning author, educator and consultant, she combines cutting edge science with spiritual philosophy to inspire holistic well-being and fullness of living. She has featured in media throughout Australia, New Zealand, Asia and the USA and regularly contributes to well-being and lifestyle publications all over the world. Born and raised in New Zealand, Kim has spent nearly half her life as a global citizen, living in Denmark, the United Kingdom, Singapore, Malaysia and Australia.

www.kimforrester.net